NEW WORKBOOK OF BASIC WRITING SKILLS

SECOND EDITION

NEW WORKBOOK OF BASIC WRITING SKILLS

SECOND EDITION

Cora L. Robey • Sarah E. Kreps • Helen M. Maloney
Tidewater Community College
Frederick Campus

Alice M. Hedrick • Ethelyn H. Morgan
Late of Tidewater Community College
Frederick Campus

HARCOURT BRACE JOVANOVICH, PUBLISHERS
San Diego New York Chicago Washington, D.C. Atlanta
London Sydney Toronto

ISBN: 0-15-565722-4

Library of Congress Catalog Card Number: 83-81133
Printed in the United States of America

Preface

The *New Workbook of Basic Writing Skills*, Second Edition, provides practice in the fundamentals of English. It includes a wide range of step-by-step exercises in sentence construction, spelling and punctuation, usage, paragraph development, the preparation of a full-length paper, and business letter writing.

The *Workbook* follows the format of the companion *New Handbook of Basic Writing Skills*, Second Edition; however, it may be used just as effectively in conjunction with another handbook or as an independent text. Although the exercises cover all the areas of the traditional handbooks, special emphasis is given to the problems that trouble beginning writers—particularly verb endings, subject-verb agreement, noun plurals, possessive endings, sentence fragments, run-together sentences, and sentence sense. Since problems vary from student to student, exercises may be assigned individually. The book may also be used for review by an entire class.

The Second Edition of the *Workbook* has added traditional grammatical terminology, but we have tried to keep that terminology simple. The explanations are easy to understand, and the exercises—many of them drawn from the actual work of our students—are realistic and vivid. The *Workbook*, like the *Handbook*, has added or improved its treatment of the following subjects:

1. *this–these* confusion
2. phrase and clause fragments
3. comma splices
4. *good* and *well*
5. the *who–whom* confusion
6. the passive and some uses of the subjunctive
7. subject and object pronouns
8. change of person
9. spelling errors caused by vowel–*r* reversal
10. spelling errors caused by miscounting syllables
11. the parts of speech, including lists of pronouns and conjunctions
12. unnecessary use of the semicolon
13. tense sequence
14. clichés and jargon
15. introductory rhetorical techniques (brainstorming, editing, and outlining)

An Instructor's Manual is available and contains diagnostic tests and answers to all exercises in both the *Handbook* and *Workbook.*

We have missed the talents, energy, and friendship of our co-authors, Alice M. Hedrick and Ethelyn H. Morgan, who died just before we began our work on this edition. We wish to thank our editors at Harcourt Brace Jovanovich and our colleagues at Tidewater Community College, Frederick Campus, for their assistance and advice during the preparation of the *Workbook.*

Cora L. Robey
Sarah E. Kreps
Helen M. Maloney

Contents

SPELLING AND PUNCTUATION

WORDS

MOVING TOWARD THE COMPLETE PAPER

THE COMPLETE PAPER

CHAPTER ONE

Sentence Makeup

1a
What is a sentence?

1-1 Beginning and ending sentences correctly

Directions: The following groups of words are sentences, but they do not look like sentences. Make corrections by starting each sentence with a capital letter and ending each one with a period, a question mark, or an exclamation point.

Example: my friend Linda loves to play the piano.

1. most people make decisions every day

2. autumn is usually a beautiful time of year

3. do you like to play basketball

4. that was a wild party

5. the entire community should be concerned about dangerous intersections

1-2 Recognizing sentences

Directions: The following is a group of sentences not separated by punctuation. As you copy it, start each sentence with a capital letter and end each one with a period, question mark, or exclamation point. There are seven sentences.

after working five days, I look forward to the weekend I collect my camping gear and head for two days of fun and relaxation when I arrive at the campgrounds, I walk around to see if any of my friends are there then I go for a swim after dark, I build a fire and make plans for the next day when the weekend is over, I am rested, refreshed, and ready to go to work again why don't you enjoy a camping trip soon

____

____

____

____

____

____

____

____

____

____

1-3 Recognizing parts of speech

Directions: As you read the following paragraph, decide the part of speech of each underlined word. Then write the appropriate word from the list below in the blank line at the right.

NOUN	PRONOUN	VERB	ADJECTIVE
ADVERB	PREPOSITION	CONJUNCTION	ARTICLE

Jogging is my favorite outdoor activity. I like it not only because jogging keeps me in good physical condition, but also because as I jog, I become familiar with my neighborhood and can now see the whole scene. I notice the effects of the changing seasons on the houses and yards that I pass. I see many of the same people (and dogs) every day. This helps me to know the people of my neighborhood, so that I feel more a part of it. In addition my muscles are firm. I sleep better and I have lost fifteen pounds already. The benefits of jogging are so many that I look forward eagerly to my daily routine.

____
____
____
____
____
____
____
____
____
____

1b
Recognize the subject and verb.

1-4 Locating verbs

Directions: In the following sentences the subject is underlined once. Underline the verb twice. Then write both underlined words in the blanks at the right.

	Subject	*Verb*
Example: We hear a great deal today about child abuse.	We	hear
1. Children like being praised, too	______	______
2. My own experience has taught me many things.	______	______
3. Good nutrition requires good eating habits.	______	______
4. Students are expected to use their dictionaries.	______	______
5. Joe believes in studying three hours every day.	______	______

6. Parades have been known to last as long as four hours. ________ ________

1-5 *Locating subjects*

Directions: In the following sentences the verb is underlined twice. Underline the subject once. Then write both underlined words in the blanks at the right.

Subject *Verb*

Example: The police should enforce the law. police should enforce

1. In order to pass the test, you should study the assigned material. ________ ________
2. My dancing class meets every Tuesday afternoon. ________ ________
3. That house by the side of the road belongs to my aunt. ________ ________
4. Children can easily learn folk dancing. ________ ________
5. Michelle tried out for cheerleading. ________ ________
6. Nonviolent protest marches were organized by Dr. Martin Luther King, Jr. ________ ________

1-6 *Locating verbs*

Directions: In the following sentences the subject is underlined once. Underline the verb twice. Then write both underlined words in the blanks at the right.

Subject *Verb*

Example: All of the students seemed as anxious as I. All seemed

1. My approach to others is friendly. ________ ________
2. Some of the equipment used in today's schools includes TV and stereo sets. ________ ________
3. The lights in our house are attached to timers. ________ ________

4. My brother, in spite of all my efforts, refused to take my best friend to the dance. ________ ________

5. The study of environmental problems is rewarding. ________ ________

6. Things such as historical sites, sandy beaches, and modern entertainment centers make our area interesting. ________ ________

7. Mr. Tucker, the festival organizer, promised an entirely new amusement area for this year's event. ________ ________

8. By following directions carefully, you save time. ________ ________

9. Joel Switz, winner of this year's aware for safe driving, has been a stock car racer for years. ________ ________

10. The opening of the drawbridge stopped the flow of traffic. ________ ________

1-7 Locating subjects

Directions: In the following sentences the verb is underlined twice. Underline the subject once. Then write the subject and verb in the blanks at the right.

	Subject	*Verb*
Example: There is very little time for homework.	time	is
1. Here are all the examples in this book.	________	________
2. There by the side of the road is his golf ball.	________	________
3. Here and there on the paper appeared a few words.	________	________
4. There are three major steps in making any garment.	________	________
5. Where is your dictionary?	________	________
6. There is no order to his paper.	________	________

7. Over the living-room couch hangs my favorite picture. ________ ________

8. All over the floor lay the spilled contents of my sewing basket. ________ ________

9. Across the railroad tracks and around the corner stands my house. ________ ________

10. Where has all the money gone? ________ ________

1-8 Locating subjects

Directions: In the following sentences the verb is underlined twice. If the subject is given in the sentence, underline it once, and write both underlined words in the blanks at the right. If the subject is understood, write *you* in the first blank and the verb in the second.

	Subject	*Verb*
Example: No matter what happens, get home by twelve o'clock.	you	get
1. Go to the next sentence.	________	________
2. Television sometimes distracts me.	________	________
3. Collect all your material carefully.	________	________
4. Smoke only in the smoking areas.	________	________
5. Throw your line far out into the water.	________	________
6. Unexpected interruptions kept me from completing the assignment.	________	________
7. Please close the door quietly.	________	________
8. Drop everything and come immediately.	________	________
	________	________

9. When cutting out a dress, lay the pattern on the fabric carefully. _________ _________

10. Develop your paragraph by adding several sentences. _________ _________

1-9 Locating main verbs in independent clauses

Directions: The following sentences each have more than one subject and more than one verb. The main subject is underlined once. Underline the main verb twice. Then write both underlined words in the blanks at the right.

	Subject	*Verb*
Example: Whenever the baby is hungry, she cries.	she	cries
1. Whenever Jennie pins the dress pattern to the fabric, she keeps the pins in the seam line.		
2. Although I don't know the exact number, many people were at the party.		
3. My mother always fixes a big meal when we have guests.		
4. My paragraphs are usually too short even though I try to explain everything.		
5. No customers came to my brother's lemonade stand although he had everything ready.		

1-10 Locating subjects and verbs in sentences joined by **and** *or* **but**

Directions: The following sentences have two independent clauses that are joined by *and* or *but.* Each independent clause contains a subject and a verb. Draw one line under each subject and two lines under each verb. Then write the underlined words in the blanks at the right.

	Subject	*Verb*
Example: Once our dog bit him, and after that the mailman refused to deliver our mail.	dog	bit
	mailman	refused
1. My friend's name is Ralph, and he lives in Syracuse.	________	________
	________	________
2. Not only did I forget my books, but I also forgot my lunch.	________	________
	________	________
3. My brother had a good report card, but my grades were only fair.	________	________
	________	________
4. My father works in the shipyard and my mother keeps house for us.	________	________
	________	________
5. My home is in the country, but I enjoy visiting friends in the city.	________	________
	________	________

1-11 Review

Directions: Copy the following paragraph, underlining the simple subjects of the complete sentences once and the main verbs that go with them twice. Do not underline the subject and verb of any incomplete part. Some sentences have more than one main verb.

Every day our reading class meets at 9:15 A.M. As soon as we get to the classroom, we go to our seats, open our books, and begin that day's work. Sometimes everyone in the class reads his own assigned material; sometimes we all discuss a book or story that we have read. The instructor changes the routine as much as possible. However, we spend most of the time reading because we believe that practice is a good way of improving our reading skills.

____

____

____

____

____

____

____

____

____

____

1c
Write correct negative sentences.

1-12 Finding negative words

Directions: In the following sentences circle each word that makes a sentence negative. Then write the negative word in the blank at the right.

Example: Some people (never) learn from mistakes. never

1. I am never going there again. ______________

2. There was nothing in the sky, but the terrible noise seemed to be right above the building. ______________

3. We called and ran from room to room, but the child was nowhere in the house. ______________

4. Many people believe that there is no such thing as a witch. ______________

5. Do not use the spot remover until you have read the directions. ______________

6. I can hardly hear you. ______________

1-13 Finding contractions of the verb with **not**

Directions: Find the word that includes the contraction of *not* and circle the word. Then write the circled word as it would be if not shortened or contracted.

Example: The work on the car (wasn't) finished, and we had to go by bus. was not

1. Marvin couldn't take his dog with him. ______________

2. It isn't easy to laugh at yourself. ______________

3. After people became aware of the pollution problem, they didn't throw trash into the lake. ______________

4. Please don't bring all of those boxes in here. ______________

5. The school wasn't notified that the meeting had been canceled. ______________

1-14 Using negative words

Directions: The following sentences have too many negative words. Correct the sentences by rewriting and leaving out one negative word or by substituting *ever* for *never* or by substituting *any* for *no* or *none*. Remember that *hardly* is a negative word.

Examples: They never see no reason for changing methods.

Sentence corrected by leaving out a negative word:

They see no reason for changing methods.

Sentence corrected by substituting *any* for *no*:

They never see any reason for changing methods.

1. None of the men want no work of that kind. ______________________

____

2. I didn't eat none of the cake. ______________________

____

3. They didn't never know the difference between the jobs. ______________________

____

4. There wasn't never candy enough for all of us. ______________________

____

5. You can't have a good marriage no other way. ______________________

____

6. The men can't hardly move those heavy boxes. ______________________

____

7. She has not never had any confidence in herself. ______________________

____

8. Never let no child go out by himself in a small boat. ______________________

____

9. You can't never leave out the last step if you want the job to turn out right. ______

____

____

10. We never heard no whistle, and we had to walk all the way home. ____________

____

11. I am not going to do neither of those things. ____________

____

12. Is it true that hardly nobody cares about that book? ____________

____

1d
Use singular and plural nouns correctly.

1-15 Using singular and plural nouns

Directions: In the sentences below draw one line under any incorrect singular or plural noun. Then write that word correctly in the blank at the right.

Example: A slip-on shoes is sometimes called a loafer. shoe

1. All kind of people enjoy a parade. ____________
2. Every days of my life I begin a new adventure. ____________
3. One days Sam will probably get all of the answers right. ____________
4. After the show some peoples stood around talking to each other. ____________
5. Add the liquid slowly, a spoonful at a times. ____________
6. If you follow these direction carefully, you will be able to make your own dress. ____________
7. As the result of a long training periods, he became skilled in the sport. ____________

8. A sofa is one of the most important item in a living room. ______

9. My club has members from every kinds of background. ______

10. Sometimes life in the army can be very exciting for a certain groups of people. ______

1-16 Locating nouns that should be plural

Directions: The sentences below contain incorrectly used nouns. Underline any of these nouns that you find. Then write each underlined noun correctly in the blank at the right.

Example: I tried to enroll in that course three time. *times*

1. I prefer American cars over all other on the market. ______
2. Three week later than I had planned, I left for New York. ______
3. Holiday time was busy, with plenty of thing to do. ______
4. To get to school very easily, follow these few simple direction. ______
5. Almost every Saturday night I really enjoy attending dance at private clubs. ______
6. My sister has so many clothes that she has trouble choosing which of her dress to wear. ______
7. Being with my friends makes my weekend happy ones. ______
8. Playing cards with other student in the cafeteria is fun for me. ______
9. Four ambulance took the injured passengers to the nearest hospital. ______
10. Sometimes babies don't like to wear shoe. ______

1-17 Recognizing words that mean more than one person, thing, or idea

Directions: In the following sentences cross out the noun (in parentheses) that is used incorrectly. Then write the correct word in the blank at the right.

Example: That tablet now costs ninety-eight (~~cent~~, cents). cents

1. I've tried to work that arithmetic problem at least five (time, times). ________
2. All of John's (friend, friends) feel the same way about the problem as he does. ________
3. Nightclub singers often include a sad (song, songs) in their acts. ________
4. On many (occasion, occasions) traffic has been heavy on Interstate 95. ________
5. College classes sometimes include a few older (student, students). ________
6. We can't expect to be right at every (period, periods) of our lives. ________
7. To make that blouse you will need five (yard, yards) of material. ________
8. (Sometime, Sometimes) the work is just too difficult. ________
9. People laugh at some of Jane's (excuse, excuses). ________
10. After a few weak (attempt, attempts) at studying, Bill gave up and went out with his friends. ________

1-18 Locating nouns that have special plural forms

Directions: In the following sentences cross out the noun (in parentheses) that is used incorrectly. Then write the correct work in the blank at the right.

Example: Our living room is twenty (foot, feet) wide. feet

1. Being cruel to (childs, children) is called child abuse. ________________
2. The kinds of work some (womans women) can do are limited by law in some states. ________________
3. Usually Marvin finds it very easy to carry on conversations with other (mans, men). ________________
4. Sometimes high-school (freshman, freshmen) outnumber the seniors. ________________
5. He couldn't believe his eyes when he passed a (women, woman) working on the road-building project. ________________
6. Dentists usually advise people to brush their (tooths, teeth) carefully at least twice a day. ________________
7. Usually the (foremans, foremen) at large industrial plants have authority over some other employees. ________________
8. Every fall many (goose, geese) fly over our area on their way to marshy lands farther south. ________________
9. He covered his cold (feets, feet). ________________

1-19 Using nouns that have no plural forms

Directions: In the sentences below cross out the noun (in parentheses) that is used incorrectly. Then write the correct work in the blank at the right.

Example: The world really needs (love, loves). love

1. Every fall my brother and I go to the Dismal Swamp to hunt (deer, deers). ______________

2. Raising (sheeps, sheep) is not a very important farming occupation in southern Virginia. ______________

3. Many pounds of (salmon, salmons) are eaten every year by people throughout the world. ______________

4. Modern schools have all kinds of (equipment, equipments). ______________

5. Sam told me that his favorite way to spend his weekends is with (peoples, people). ______________

6. There are several reasons for (angers, anger). ______________

1-20 Using nouns correctly

Directions: As you read the following paragraph, decide which of the nouns are incorrectly used. Cross out those nouns and write the correct forms above.

Example: My sister is afraid of ~~mouses~~ *mice*.

It hardly seems possible that so many years have passed since I lived on a farm and took care of goose, horses, and sheeps. Doing this things was great fun for me because I enjoyed being so close to nature. In my spare time I sometimes hunted. Rabbits and quails were plentiful in the forest nearby. Fishes, too, were abundant in the creek that flowed through the farm. Sometimes I caught trouts, and sometimes I caught basses. Whatever came to my hook was welcome. As I remember this times of my life, I think that it was the best time of all.

1-21 Review

Directions: Copy the paragraph below, correcting any errors in the use of nouns.

Several thing in my high-school career pleased me. Many of the class were pleasant as well as informative. Almost every teachers was helpful and interested in each students. Only a few peoples ever had any real trouble with classwork. The assembly program were usually entertaining and interesting. After schools all kind of sports activities were held. There were even several other thing to do One of the nearby school opened its pool to permit different age group to swim at different times. Maybe I didn't like school all the times because I couldn't decide whether some young man and woman were there to study or to play.

CHAPTER TWO

Incomplete Sentences

2a

Complete a fragment that has no subject or verb.

2-1 Correcting fragments

Directions: Correct each fragment by joining it to a complete sentence next to it Then write each sentence you have changed in the blank provided. Look especially for groups of words beginning with *as, in, into, from, to, with,* and *without.*

Example: I told him to put all the books down. On the table. I told him to put all the books down on the table.

1. Back in high school my courses were easy, and I could make B's and C's. Without much effort. ____

2. I decided that if I ever try snorkeling again, I should try under much more suitable conditions. With my own equipment, low tide, and five more lessons. ____

3. We spent our vacation catching trout. And frequently bass. And sometimes just waiting for a fish to bite. ____

____

____

4. She usually dresses in the latest style. With jewelry, shoes, and bag to match. ________

____

5. I believe Nancy is the best friend I have. She will always help me. In any way possible. I consider her a special kind of friend. ______________________________

____

____

6. Jamie was almost two years old before he learned how to walk. Now I can hardly keep up with him. He is constantly running around, getting into trouble. His energy lasts. From morning until night. ______________________________

____

____

____

7. Martin is usually fifteen minutes late to pick me up, but he complains if I am even one minute late. He ends up rushing to get to school before roll is taken. In his first class. ______________________________________

____

____

____

8. I finally saw the ship coming in. As it was getting closer, three tugboats appeared.

They went to their respective places. With one tugboat in front, one in back, and one on the side. ____________________

____

____

____

9. You can learn to do a handstand if you have proper body position. With your hands shoulder-width apart, your legs and back straight, and your toes pointed. Do not let your shoulders sink in. Practice against a wall to gain confidence. ____________________

____

____

____

2-2 Correcting prepositional phrase fragments

Directions: Turn each fragment into a complete sentence.

Example: by the lake We stayed in a cabin by the lake.

1. against my advice ____________________
2. after breakfast ____________________
3. beside the building on the right ____________________

   ____
4. during the spring ____________________
5. into the deep end of the pool ____________________

   ____
6. from Vermont to California ____________________

   ____

7. as soon as possible ______________________________

____

8. to the movies ______________________________

9. with three of my friends ______________________________

____

10. by walking away ______________________________

11. through the window with a crash ______________________________

____

12. without any concern for others ______________________________

____

13. in front of the school theater ______________________________

____

14. by my apartment window ______________________________

____

15 as a lifeguard for the summer ______________________________

____

16. with a slight breeze blowing ______________________________

____

17. to the best school in the area ______________________________

____

2-3 Completing phrase fragments

Directions: Rewrite the following paragraph, eliminating all fragments.

You may wake up one morning and discover you have slept too long. Not leaving yourself enough time to get ready for work. Here are some simple suggestions. For getting dressed and on your way. In ten exciting minutes. Spring out of bed. Checking your calendar to be sure it isn't Sunday. Proceed to the bathroom. Grabbing your towel, washcloth, and clean underwear as you go. Turn on the shower. While ripping off your pajamas. Jump into the shower. Being careful not to slip on the wet floor. Soap your body. Dumping shampoo onto your hair. After rinsing well. Turn off the shower and dry yourself. Brush your hair and apply deodorant. At the same time. Then get dressed. Not bothering to dry your hair You can do this on the way to work. By hanging your head out of the car window. The car is also a good place. For applying makeup. Especially at traffic lights. These suggestions should help you. On the next morning that you oversleep.

2b
Correct a dependent clause fragment.

2-4 Correcting dependent clause fragments

Directions: Eliminate each fragment by joining the dependent clause to a main clause next to it. Decide whether it should come before or after the main clause. Then write each sentence you have changed. If you put the fragment first, insert a comma after it.

Example: We left without him. Because he was late. We left without him because he was late.

1. I ran into a parked car. My cousin sat a few minutes and then got out to see whom the car belonged to. Even though the car wasn't damaged.

2. Although it was raining. We went to the picnic. ______________________________

____

3. In the city there are more job opportunities. Because it is larger and has more stores and factories. ______________________________

____

____

4. When my alarm went off at seven o'clock this morning. I had to jump right out of bed. I had a lot to do before school. ______________________________

____

____

5. My cousin tried to find me a job. Because I had graduated from high school and wasn't planning to go to college for a while. ______________________________

____

____

6. After you remove the hamburger from the oven. Pour the creamed potatoes over it. Then sit down to a delicious meal. ______________________________

____

____

7. Although my idea of the ideal mate has changed some. I still think it is important to marry someone who has the same goals as I do. ______________________________

____

____

8. Bath time is an ideal family time. Because a baby is most alert, receptive, and responsive at this time. ____________________

____

____

9. After you wet your hair. Put the shampoo on and rub it in well. Repeat this process and rinse thoroughly. Until your hair has no trace of soap in it. ____________________

____

____

10. Everyone spent the next three hours dancing. While I just sat there and watched. And I tried to figure out the steps so I could teach them to Jerry. ____________________

____

____

11. When they start playing some of those songs. You can't sit still and just listen. The music makes you want to dance, too. Even if you don't know how. ____________________

____

____

____

12. Although I thought I would be too tired to have a good time. I must admit that I was glad I went to The Seawall with the others. It was more fun than I'd expected because we all went together. And because there were other people to dance with.

____

____

____

2-5 *Using* **because, when, after, as, although, since, even though,** ***and*** **while**

Directions: Make a complete sentence out of each of the following fragments. Whenever the fragment comes first, put a comma after it.

Example: because it was raining *I had to stay indoors because it was raining.*

1. because I was too tired ______________________________

2. when the music starts to play ______________________________

3. after we got home from the trip ______________________________

4. as he walked down the street ______________________________

5. although I started as a business major ______________________________

6. after we had shopped for three hours ______________________________

7. because I am a full-time student ______________________________

8. even though he swims better than I ______________________________

9. because I did so well on the test ______________________________

10. while I am talking on the telephone ______________________

____

2-6 Correcting relative (dependent) clause fragments

Directions: Correct each fragment by joining it to a sentence next to it.

Example: I have four brothers. Who are all younger than I. I have four brothers who are all younger than I.

1. My friend Barbara is a sweet person. Who has not changed much over the years. ______

____

____

2. That trip was one I will always remember. We saw many interesting places. Which I could talk about for years. ______________________

____

____

3. A friend is a person who is around when you need help. Who will do almost anything for you. ______________________

____

4. Inside the house is a set of old colonial furniture that I like. Which reminds me of the olden days. ______________________

____

____

5. She taught me that I could stand on my own feet. That life itself was a gift with certain rules, and that my conscience was there to help me follow the rules. ______

____

6. My friend married a natural athlete. Who is good at every sport she tries. ___________

7. Some people define love as an attraction to another person. Who is of the opposite sex. Most people would agree with that, but there is more you should know about love. ___________

8. At night Paris is beautiful, with bright lights. That outline some of the city buildings.

2-7 Correcting relative clause fragments

Directions: Make complete sentences using the following fragments. Use commas where needed.

Example: who is twelve years old My cousin, who is twelve years old, is visiting me.

1. who is my neighbor ___________

2. that sits in the corner ___________

3. which hangs in front of the kitchen window ______________________________

____

4. which cost $25 ______________________________

____

5. who comes from Pittsburgh ______________________________

____

6. which took three years to build ______________________________

____

7. that is painted blue and white ______________________________

____

8. which is a luxury car ______________________________

____

9. who is an excellent pianist ______________________________

____

10. who raises German shepherds for a living ______________________________

____

2c
Correct a verb fragment.

2-8 Correcting verb fragments

Directions: Eliminate each fragment by joining it to a complete sentence next to it. Write each sentence you have changed.

Example: I read two chapters of history. And wrote my English theme. I read two chapters of history and wrote my English theme.

1. My sister and I share clothes, jewelry, and books And often share boyfriends, too.

2. To succeed in school you must budget your time wisely, eat right, and get enough sleep. And study hard.

3. Vanessa usually comes to school by bus. But sometimes catches a ride with a friend.

4. John Wilson is a safe, considerate driver who is careful to observe the speed limit. He watches for unseen hazards. And always lets other drivers have the right-of-way.

5. Frank frequently let the water in his car battery get too low. And never got new tires until he couldn't pass inspection with his bald ones. He also drove with a badly cracked windshield for ten months.

6. I rushed to get ready to go to the movie. But didn't get there until it had already

started. I had to stay after the end to catch the first ten minutes of the next showing.

7. For five years my cousin has worked as a receptionist for a doctor. And has worked as a nurse's aide too. Now she wants to go to nursing school to become a registered nurse.

2d
Correct a noun fragment.

2-9 Correcting noun fragments

Directions: Correct each noun fragment by rewriting it or by joining it to a sentence next to it. If you join it to a sentence, use a comma (,) or colon (:) between them when the sentence comes first. When the fragment comes first, use a dash (–).

Examples: That is what I have always wanted. A room of my own. What I have always wanted is a room of my own. That is what I've always wanted: a room of my own.

A room of my own. That is what I have always wanted. A room of my own is what I have always wanted. A room of my own—that is what I have always wanted.

1. I was ready to enjoy my meal. The rare meat cooked just as I wanted it. The wine

was chilled perfectly. ______________________________

____

2. There are two kinds of skating. Roller skating and ice skating. ______________

____

3. There are several main factors in skating. Momentum, direction, and lean. All three are important. ______________________________

____

4. There are three pattern pieces to the pants. The front, the back, and the waistband.

____

____

5. Independence Day is a day to have a family cookout. A day to stay home from school. A day to do nothing but just be lazy. ______________________________

____

____

6. I'm standing on a small hill above a village. The view of the village is most delightful. The cozy little inns with beautiful and colorful designs around the windows down below me. ______________________________

____

____

____

7. We had a special dinner out to celebrate. Prime rib, baked potato, salad, wine, coffee, and cheesecake. I ate enough to make two meals. ______________________________

____

____

8. We must think about our future together. The house, the children, and a place to live where we can be happy. ______________________________

____

____

9. A gymnast must have the proper attire. A leotard so she can move freely and gymnastic shoes. The shoes should have rubber soles so they do not slide. ______________________________

____

____

____

10. It was exactly what I had wanted. A job as lifeguard at the pool for the summer. However, I hardly ever got to use the pool myself. ______________________________

____

____

____

11. They have rules that must be obeyed. Rules such as the proper time to come in and days for washing dishes and washing clothes. ______________________________

____

____

____

12. Mrs. Barrows had an unusual laugh. A laugh that made her sound more like a donkey than a person. ______________________________

____

____

2e
Correct an infinitive fragment.

2-10 Correcting infinitive fragments

Directions: Correct infinitive and other fragments by joining them to complete sentences next to them. Then write each new sentence in the blank provided. If the fragment comes before the complete sentence, put a comma after it.

Example: I made a resolution. To try my best. I made a resolution to try my best.

1. We all ran to the windows. To see what all the commotion was about. The neighbor's dog had chased our two cats up a tree. And both were scolding him loudly. ________

2. His life is filled with interesting experiences. He got comfortable at the table. To talk about them in great detail We all listened until midnight. ________

3. I recall standing on the corner where everyone gathered on a warm summer's night. To play hide-and-seek. This was one of the best times of my childhood. I can remember the names of the people who lived on our street and liked to sit on their porches in the evenings. ________

4. To get the best mileage from your car. Try to avoid fast starts and driving over 55 miles per hour. Having your car properly tuned can also help. ______________

5. I sent out over thirty letters to companies in the area. To try to get a summer job that did not involve night work. After a few weeks I was called for the first interview. To see if I was the sort of worker needed. I was nervous when answering the questions asked but got the job anyway. ______________

6. Training beyond high school is almost essential. To help you get a responsible job that you will really enjoy. Just making money is not enough to satisfy you if the work is boring. ______________

7. To prepare for your job interview. Dress conservatively and neatly and have a résumé with you. To help you in filling out the application. And to jog your memory when answering questions. Even if a lot of the same information is required on the application, having a résumé is a good idea. You should check it over periodically. To make sure it is up to date. And to list information such as recent courses you have taken.

8. Raising a child can give a woman a sense of responsibility. And the father is now participating more actively in child-rearing. Not only to help out if the wife works outside the home. But also to have more influence on his children's lives. He realizes how important he is to them. To his daughters as well as his sons. He is the main male role model as his children grow up. The father can be as much a parent as the mother. He can help his children to grow up without feeling he was never at home. To help them out when they need him. And to give the guidance only a father can give. To experience all the rewards of being a parent a man has to get involved. And not think that being with children is women's work.

2-11 Review

Directions: Rewrite the following paragraph, correcting each fragment by joining it to a complete sentence next to it.

Sir Arthur Conan Doyle was a British novelist and storyteller. Best known for his stories about Sherlock Holmes. Who is a famous detective. Dr. Watson is a friend of Holmes. Helping him whenever he can. Watson is always surprised at the clues Holmes manages to find. Because he isn't as smart as Holmes. I enjoy seeing if I can solve Holmes' cases before he reveals the solution. It is a simple matter of putting pieces together. In their proper order. It is like finishing a jigsaw puzzle. Being finally able to see the whole picture. I am able to figure out more than Watson. Who is always two steps behind. But usually I have to wait until the last chapter. To see how Holmes solves the case. There is an element of suspense. To make me wonder how he will find the clue he needs.

CHAPTER THREE

Run-Together Sentences and Comma Splices

3a
Separate your sentences by using a period.

3-1 Separating run-together sentences or comma splices with a period

Directions: The following sentences have not been separated (a run-together sentence) or are separated only by a comma (a comma splice). Rewrite each pair of sentences. End the first sentence with a period and begin the next sentence with a capital letter.

Example: Her hair is very white, it reminds me of fresh, white snow. Her hair is very white. It reminds me of fresh, white snow.

1. Jerry has a very good voice and plays the piano well with his musical talent he should consider majoring in music. ______________________

2. The camel travels many miles across the desert with heavy loads on its back it is the only animal that can be used for desert transportation. ______________________

3. She asked if he wanted to go to the movie he didn't want to go. ______

4. The drugstore is the most convenient store in the neighborhood, usually it opens early in the morning and stays open until late in the evening. ______

5. In class listen and ask questions about things you don't understand the teacher will explain as well as he or she can. ______

6. After you have looked at the tires, shake a wheel on the front if it moves in and out, the car needs new wheel bearings. ______

7. Gasoline, propane, and diesel fuel are used to provide power for vehicles, as our population increases, we need to find new sources of energy besides coal and petroleum. ______

8. It was a perfect day for fishing we collected our poles and other gear and set off for

a relaxing afternoon. ____

____

____

9. As my radio fills the air with beautiful music, my whole world becomes a dream there are no more tears to shed, no more anxiety or depression, no more cold or rainy days. ____

____

____

____

10. A beautiful lawn doesn't just happen by accident it is the result of many hours of work and much careful planning. ____

____

____

3b
Separate your sentences by using a semicolon.

3-2 Using a semicolon

Directions: Correct the following run-together sentences and comma splices by using a semicolon. Remember to add commas where needed.

Example: He was fifteen minutes late for class, therefore he missed the directions for the test. *He was fifteen minutes late for class; therefore, he missed the directions for the test.*

1. I had hoped to have a nap before I made dinner, however there wasn't time. ________

____

____

2. Sheila and I are about the same size, we both wear size 12. ________

____

____

3. Jerry spent two hours each night this week studying for the history test, therefore, he is confident that he will pass it. ________

____

____

4. We enjoyed the carefully prepared meal in elegant surroundings, then we sat and relaxed over coffee and dessert. ________

____

____

5. Mark has a good sense of humor, everyone enjoys the jokes he tells. ________

____

____

6. June is qualified for the job, moreover she has had experience in that field. ________

____

____

7. I have known Martin for many years in fact he is one of my closest friends. ________

____

____

8. I found it hard to pay attention during the last speaker's presentation, he spoke in a monotone and appeared to ramble. ______

______

______

9. Today was a very productive day I got all my work done for the next two days, washed my car, and wrote three letters to friends. ______

______

______

10. I find it difficult to enjoy grocery shopping, in fact, I put it off as long as I can. ______

______

______

3c
Separate your sentences by using a comma and a coordinating conjunction such as *and, but, or, nor, for, so,* or *yet*.

3-3 Separating run-together sentences

Directions: The following sentences are not separated at all or are separated only by a comma or by a coordinating conjunction without a comma. Correct the sentences by using both a comma and *and, but, or, nor, for, so,* or *yet.* Remember to use the comma before the conjunction.

Example: The supervisor oversees all operations, he makes the decisions for the workers under him. The supervisor oversees all operations, and he makes the decisions for the workers under him.

1. Just inside the room is a large desk, to the left is the door to the supply room. ______

____

____

2. I had heard of such things happening to other people I couldn't believe it was happening to me. ______________________________

____

____

3. Lay the pattern pieces out correctly you can waste material if you are not careful.

____

____

4. I don't really enjoy baseball nor does football appeal to me. ______________

____

____

5. Rinse the hair several times it will not shine unless all of the shampoo is removed.

____

____

6. My next-door neighbor buys beautiful clothes but she doesn't like to take care of them. ______________________________________

____

____

7. They will deliver the things you buy right to your home you can see and try the products before you pay for them. ______________________

____

____

8. I like to clean house and rearrange things, while I am working, I listen to music.

9. Larry had to miss class on Monday, he asked a friend in the class to take notes for him.

10. I like to listen to a good rock group everyone in my family enjoys the same type of music.

3d
Separate your sentences by making one of them a dependent clause.

3-4 Separating run-together sentences

Directions: Correct the following run-together sentences by turning the last one in each pair into a dependent clause, using *before, after, when, because,* or *since.*

Example: The scenery finally became interesting we came to a beautiful park.

The scenery finally became interesting when we came to a beautiful park.

1. He looked really well-groomed he had his hair styled.

2. I didn't mind doing a favor for her she has often helped me in the past. ________

____

____

3. I ran around trying to close all of the windows the rain started to fall. ________

____

____

4. You will probably get the job you have some experience in similar work. ________

____

____

5. I had to review only two hours for the exam I had spent a few minutes after each class going over my notes. ________________________

____

____

6. We will have a test on the first part of the course we have completed a review.

____

____

7. It is surprising that Gordon is so tall his mother and father are of only average height.

____

____

8. The tree on the corner of the street fell over into our yard a huge truck hit it.

____

____

9. I think I can reach my goal of a college degree I am trying to do the best work that I

can in all of my classes. ______________________________

____

____

10. Air and water pollution are problems that all of us should be concerned about we all want comfortable, healthy areas for our homes. ______________________________

____

____

____

3e
Avoid the comma splice. Do not use a comma alone to separate your sentences.

3-5 Avoiding comma splices

Directions: The following sentences are separated only by a comma. This is an error called a comma splice. Change the comma into a semicolon or a period followed by a capital letter.

Example: This is going to be a cold winter, we have had freezing temperatures already.

This is going to be a cold winter; we have had freezing temperatures already.

1. Reading is a way to broaden one's mind, my favorite stories are science fiction.

____

____

2. Put away the jack and the tire, now you are ready to roll. ______________________________

____

3. She wears glasses because she is nearsighted, she doesn't need to wear them when she reads. ______________________________

____

____

4. Bill's father took both of us deer hunting, my friend enjoyed it, but I didn't.

____

____

5. Don't overload the house circuits, check the fuse box for voltage requirements.

____

____

6. I'm definitely not a morning person, I prefer staying up half the night and then sleeping until noon the next day. ______________________________

____

____

7. I am undecided about a career, I plan to transfer to a four-year university in the fall, though. ______________________________

____

____

8. Yes, my major is biology, I am extremely interested in the medical field and hope to find my life's work in that area. ______________________________

____

____

9. Seeing huge mountains for the first time would probably be exciting for anyone, for

me it was a dream come true. ____

10. I'd had that dog since she was a puppy, in fact, she was the only one left from the original litter. ____

3-6 Review

Directions: Separate the following run-together sentences and comma splices by any of the methods used in the previous exercises on run-together sentences.

1. On weekends she opens her beauty shop, she has many of the women in the neighborhood as customers. ____

2. My brother, who is a postal clerk, has two sons one is a professional basketball player, and the other is in college but has not yet made a career decision. ________

3. Some people think they are sisters, they look very much alike. ______________

4. Jay is a serious student, he comes to class on time and always sits in the front of the

room and pays attention. ______________________________

____

____

5. If prisoners have behaved properly, they are put on work release, they may go outside of the prison to work. ______________________________

____

____

6. Painting a car requires skill and proper materials it is a job in which knowledge and patience go hand-in-hand. ______________________________

____

____

7. One of my friends has a wonderful voice and enjoys singing he also finds pleasure in making other people happy with his songs. ______________________________

____

____

8. You can't miss Leroy's house, it is the one with the green shutters and the six cats on the front porch. ______________________________

____

____

9. A group of people gathered signatures of concerned parents, we took the signatures to the council and asked for a traffic light at the intersection. ______________________________

____

____

____

10. In front of the couch is a white marble coffee table, in the middle of the table is an ashtray that looks like an open rhinoceros' mouth. ______________________________

____

____

____

CHAPTER FOUR

Adjectives and Adverbs

Learn to recognize adjectives (words that describe persons and things) and adverbs (words that tell how, when, and where).

4-1 Using adjectives

Directions: In the following sentences underline all adjectives. Write the underlined words in the blanks at the right.

Example: He is now very healthy and happy. *healthy* *happy*

1. Having a few pigeons, a wirehaired cat, and a fuzzy-headed dog, I own only a small part of the wild kingdom. ______ ______ ______ ______ ______

2. There are many concerned students in my classes. ______ ______

3. Although Action Community College is a smaller college, I think it is better than Gumball State. ______ ______

4. The present building seems very poorly insulated. ______ ______

5. That chair looks shapeless and feels uncomfortable. ______ ______

4-2 Using adverbs

Directions: In the following sentences underline all adverbs. Write the underlined words in the blanks at the right.

Example: That crazy man really frightened us badly. really badly

1. To do laundry properly, follow the steps listed below. ______ ______
2. Many people today are tremendously greedy. ______ ______
3. The shopping area has changed greatly just recently. ______ ______ ______
4. After waiting almost endlessly, I finally gave birth to a healthy boy. ______ ______ ______
5. The reckless drivers can be recognized easily. ______

4a
Learn participles used as adjectives.

4-3 Using past participles as adjectives

Directions: Each of the following sentences contains the present form of a verb. Turn the verb into an adjective (past participle), and write the correct work in the blank to the right. Check your dictionary, if necessary, to find the past participle of any irregular verbs.

Example: It is impossible to remove the (sink) barge. sunken

1. Remove the (loosen) lugs. ______
2. Breaking a mirror is especially unlucky when you have to pick up all the (break) glass yourself. ______

3. My mother spends all her time at the Goodwill store looking for bargains on (use) furniture. ____________

4. Carpenters become very frustrated over (bend) nails. ____________

5. I found a half- (eat) apple on the table when your sister left. ____________

6. You definitely have to cultivate a taste for (freeze) yogurt. ____________

7. Alicia didn't win, but she said the race was well (run). ____________

8. It takes an (experience) driver to handle those difficult roads. ____________

9. Cynthia has never been a very (relax) person. ____________

10. The Easter eggs are now all well (hide). ____________

4-4 Using participles as adjectives

Directions: In the following sentences cross out the incorrect words in parentheses. Write the correct words in the blanks at the right.

Example: I had a very (~~relax~~, relaxing) vacation. relaxing

1. Pour the batter into a (grease, greased) cake pan. ____________

2. My favorite chair is a big blue barrel- (shape shaped) one. ____________

3. One of the best (like, liked) courses at my university to be sociology. ____________

4. Two of the most popular types of pigeons are the king pigeon and the (fascinate, fascinating) tumbler pigeon. ____________

5. The (disturb, disturbing) phone calls woke Ida out of a sound sleep. ____________

6. (Measure, Measuring) cups should be close at hand when you are baking from scratch. ____________

7. You can often save money by buying (unfinish, unfinished) furniture. ____________

8. My sister must have a thousand pounds of (can, canned) goods in her kitchen. ____________

9. Children in an (old-fashion, old-fashioned) family were to be seen but not heard. ____________

10. (Concern, Concerned) parents should show their concern by supporting their local PTA. ____________

4-5 Using participles as adjectives

Directions: In the following sentences add *-d, -ed,* or *-ing* to any verbs used as adjectives. Write your corrections in the spaces provided at the right

Example: Going to a party is the most excit~~e~~ing thing I like to do on a weekend. exciting

1. Now tired but refresh I am ready to start again. ____________

2. On the weekends I like to go to a swing club where I can talk with friends, have a few mix drinks, and dance. ____________

3. I always open the newspaper to Ann Landers' column to get my much need chuckle. ____________

4. I love to cook scallop potatoes and meatloaf. ____________

5. I have a gold ruffle curtain in my kitchen window. ____________

6. A quarterback can get pretty discourage at times. ____________

7. In my country when a young man gains the admiration of a young woman's family, he can visit his love one with their permission. ________________

8. That was the most frighten experience I've had lately. ________________

9. Take the ruler and measure the desire length. ________________

10. She comes to class every day all dress up. ________________

4b
Use adverbs correctly.

4-6 Using adverbs

Directions: In the following sentences change adjectives to adverbs when necessary. Write the corrected form in the blank to the right.

Example: Final^ly dry the piece. Finally

1. I feel real happy about my new job. ________________

2. Tighten the lug nuts very secure so they won't come loose. ________________

3. Paul puts his clothes on different from everyone else. ________________

4. William's clothes fit him neat. ________________

5. My room is decorated very nice with bright colors. ________________

6. Wet the hair thorough. ________________

7. Swimming does not come easy to everyone. ________________

8. A considerate person won't drive too slow. ________________

9. The city council increases taxes regular. ________________

10. Harry's grandmother began lifting weights and jogging to stay physical fit. ______

4c
Use adjectives and adverbs correctly following linking verbs like *look, feel, seem, appear, taste,* and *sound.*

4-7 Using adjectives and adverbs following linking verbs

Directions: In the following sentences cross out the incorrect words in parentheses. Write the correct words in the blanks to the right.

Example: The roads appear (smooth, ~~smoothly~~). smooth

1. The dark-haired man in the doorway appeared (suspicious, suspiciously) to me. ______
2. The police appeared to be (suspicious, suspiciously) when they questioned the man. ______
3. In fact the whole street looks (differently, different). ______
4. I looked (carefully, careful) at my paper before I turned it in ______
5. Those flowers smell so (sweetly, sweet) they make me sick. ______
6. His voice sounds (flat, flatly) to me. ______
7. Susan feels (different, differently) about her father now. ______
8. Pickles and orange juice really taste (bad, badly) together. ______
9. Mr. Myers looked (sad, sadly) when he learned of his friend's illness. ______

10. Mr. Myers looked (sad, sadly) at the photo album so full of painful memories. ________________

4-8 Using adjectives and adverbs following linking verbs

Directions: In the following sentences correct any adjectives or adverbs used incorrectly after *look, feel, smell, taste, sound, seem,* and *appear.* Write the correct form of the words in the blanks at the right. Write *C* if a word is correct.

Example: Mrs. Smith, the laundry lady, appears cheerful^ly at our door every Thursday. cheerfully

1. This crabmeat doesn't smell freshly to me. ________________
2. She looked closely at his eyes to see if he was lying. ________________
3. I felt sad as I left the deserted building. ________________
4. The bells sound pretty on Sunday morning. ________________
5. That job sounded easily, but it wasn't. ________________
6. My mother felt slowly along the carpet, looking for the needle she had dropped. ________________
7. She seems friendly enough to me. ________________
8. That milk tastes and smells sourly. ________________
9. She might look sweetly, but she's not. ________________
10. His teeth make his smile look nicely. ________________

4d
Use adjectives and adverbs correctly when comparing two or more persons or things.

4-9 Using adjectives and adverbs to compare

Directions: In the following sentences cross out the incorrect describing words used to compare persons or things. Write the correct form of the words in the blanks. Write *C* if a sentence makes all comparisons correctly.

Example: As he grew ~~more~~ older, he began to eat more, stay awake longer, and cry more than he did when he was first born. older

1. The activities at the city college are at a more slower pace than the activities at the state university. ________
2. Atlanta is larger than Portsmouth. ________
3. Our den is the most coziest room of all. ________
4. The most craziest person I know is my Uncle Larry. ________
5. Of all the people I know, she is the more friendlier. ________
6. It is sometimes hard to get information across to one student than to another. ________
7. In *Death of a Salesman* there are two sons, Biff and Happy. Happy is the youngest. ________
8. My wedding day was the most wonderfulest day of my life. ________
9. The teachers at Junction College are more involved with their students than the teachers at City U. ________
10. The news made me more happier than I had ever been. ________

4e
Use *good, well, bad,* and *badly* correctly.

4-10 *Using* good, well, bad, *and* badly

Directions: In the following sentences cross out the incorrect words in parentheses. Write the correct words in the blanks to the right.

Example: If you are happy with what you are doing, you are doing (~~good~~, well). well

1. As I told my fellow choir members, whatever you do, do it (good, well). ________
2. The table should be cleaned off and wiped (good, well). ________
3. At first we didn't get along too (good, well). ________
4. Be sure to stir the mixture (good, well). ________
5. Angela has been doing (good, well) up until now. ________
6. The lightning-bolt symbol on a surfboard gives surfers status, but they could surf just as (good, well) without it. ________
7. The man in the traffic helicopter said the traffic situation was looking (good, well) that day. ________
8. I felt really (bad, badly) when you told me the news. ________
9. She had the flu yesterday but seems (good, well) today. ________
10. Alan is afraid he did (bad, badly) on his last math test. ________

4-11 Using comparative and superlative forms of good, well, bad, *and* badly

Directions: In the following sentences cross out any incorrect forms of *good, well, bad,* and *badly.* Write the correct forms. Write *C* if a word is correct.

Example: I can see why television commercials sell best than radio commercials. better

1. I have never seen a worser person than my Uncle Cal. ________
2. You shouldn't feel so badly; everybody makes mistakes. ________
3. I tried hard to do my bestest. ________
4. My brother's room is the worst mess I've ever seen. ________
5. Transfer students are treated worst than freshmen. ________
6. His cough is worse than mine. ________
7. Of the two sisters, Evelyn sings best. ________

4-12 Review

Directions: In the following sentences correct any incorrect adjectives and adverbs. Write the correct forms in the blanks to the right Write *C* if a sentence uses all adjectives and adverbs correctly.

Example: I like ice^d tea when I'm hot. iced

1. She looks seriously concerned about her work. ________
2. My sister is real polite and unselfish. ________
3. I don't know him personal, but he seems friendly. ________
4. Mr. Jones is a very quiet and lonely man. ________
5. Joe bought his car from a use car dealer. ________
6. By this time the sun was slow going down and I began to feel coldly. ________ ________

7. The houses were all real beautiful. __________

8. He is a very slow-move man who talks slow and soft __________

__________ __________

9. The roads were very bad that day. __________

10. He told me that I had a lot of burn wires under my dash- __________ board and that the wires would have to be replaced before I could drive the car safe. __________

11. I managed to look up and see the store manager give that tall red-beard man the money out of the cash register. __________

12. My doctor always washes her hands thorough and greets __________ me cheerful before she examines me. __________

13. My sister was only a year old than I was, and we were __________ both old enough to get a driver's license.

14. Wet the hair real good. __________ __________

15. My main goal is to get a well-paying job __________

4-13 Review

Directions: Copy the paragraph below, correcting any errors in the use of adjectives and adverbs.

It was a great day to play baseball. The temperature was about 80 degrees, and there was only a little breeze blowing soft. The sky was a dark blue with plenty of fluffy white clouds that shaded the field slight. The well-mark play field looked cleanly for the big game. We were all so excited about the game we couldn't wait to get on the field and start practicing early. We ran onto the field energetic; everybody seemed eagerly to play ball. Final the umpire called loud, "Play ball," and threw a ball to the tobacco-chew pitcher. We had a real good pitcher; he was striking them out as quick as they came to bat. The batters that did manage to hit balls were beaten out easy at first base. When the game ended, the score was six to nothing, our favor. That was the most happiest day I can remember for our team, but the other guys felt that it was the worsest.

CHAPTER FIVE

Subjects, Possessive Words, and Objects

5-1 Recognizing subjects, possessive words, and objects

Directions: In each blank to the right write *S, P,* or *O* to show whether the italicized word is a subject, a possessive word, or an object.

Example: *I* hardly ever cry. S

1. Leave *Mary* alone. ______________
2. Here is the book *whose* cover is torn. ______________
3. *You* are never on time. ______________
4. That new car is *mine.* ______________
5. I wrote Edna and *him* a letter. ______________
6. Let's take *our* time. ______________
7. That *boy's* jacket is torn. ______________
8. Did your mother water *her* plants? ______________
9. *Who* asked that question? ______________
10. Michael put on *his* old hat. ______________

5a

Use *I, he, she, we, they,* and *who* as subjects and *me, him, her, us, them,* and *whom* as objects.

5-2 Using subjects and objects

Directions: Decide whether each group of words should be at the beginning, in the middle, or at the end of a sentence. Then make up a sentence using the group of words in the correct position.

Example: Annie and me Alice sent Annie and me postcards.

1. she and her cousin ____________________

2. Al and I ____________________

3. he and Jane ____________________

4. us children ____________________

5. their sister and me ____________________

6. we three friends ____________________

7. Hank and him ____________________

8. to whom it belongs ____________________

5-3 *Using subjects and objects*

Directions: Cross out the incorrect pronoun(s) in parentheses in each of the following sentences. Then write the correct word or words.

Example: I wrote Ted and (~~she~~, her) a long letter her

1. George was always better than (I, me) at football. ____________
2. That night (my friends and me, my friends and I) went dancing. ____________
3. (Her, She) and her best friend were in a world of their own. ____________
4. My room is big enough for my daughter and (I, me). ____________
5. My sister is the young lady with (who, whom) you spoke.
6. She tries to use big words when (she and I, her and me) are talking. ____________
7. When I got there, (he, him) and his partner had already started. ____________
8. (We, Us) confirmed coffee drinkers never will get used to tea. ____________
9. He promised to give Sam and (I, me) a telephone call early next week. ____________
10. That is a matter entirely between you and (she, her). ____________

5b
Show possession clearly by using the correct forms.

5-4 Using possessive pronouns

Directions: Write a word that refers to the italicized subject in each of these sentences.

Example: *Julie* is certainly careless with her clothes.

1. *You and Jean* are responsible for __________ own errors.
2. My *cousins* could not find __________ way back home.
3. That *book* has lost most of __________ pages.
4. *I* think that all these jewels are __________.
5. *My sister and I* only want what is really __________.

5-5 Using possessive words

Directions: Write *C* in the blank to the right of any sentence that shows possession correctly. Rewrite any sentences that are incorrect.

Example: Is this sofa our's? Is this sofa ours?

1. Len's house is nearby. __________
2. My brother's pen is broken. __________
3. This is yours. __________
4. The dog wagged it's tail. __________

5. Mr. Allen house is at the corner of the street. ______________________________

____

6. They have their reasons. ____

____

7. It's mine's. ____

____

8. I understand Joe point of view. ____

____

9. That is their's. ____

____

10. I'm waiting for hi's answer. ____

____

5-6 *Showing possession*

Directions: Rewrite each of the following expressions, using an apostrophe to show possession.

Example: the horse of Mr. Green Mr. Green's horse

1. the mittens of my sister ______________________________
2. the aunt of Charlie ______________________________
3. the claws of the kitten ______________________________
4. the toys of the children ______________________________
5. the end of the journey ______________________________
6. the pocketbooks of the women ______________________________
7. the decision of the people ______________________________

5-7 *Showing possession*

Directions: Write *C* in the blank to the right of any sentence in which the italicized word shows possession correctly. Rewrite any sentences that show possession incorrectly.

Example: The *bus'* is not on schedule today. The bus is not on schedule today.

1. Hardwood *floor's* add to the beauty of the room. ______

2. No one can take *Edna's* place. ______

3. The *author's* tone seems very cynical. ______

4. A large mat *hang's* over the chair. ______

5. My son is always leaving his *sweater's* at school. ______

6. The game lies in the *quarterback's* hands. ______

7. Relocation *improve's* some *people's* lifestyles. ______

8. Several *year's* ago, I enrolled in *paratroopers'* school. ______

9. Please call the *Registrar's* office for information. ______

10. Her three *son's* were all good students. ____________________

____

5-8 Showing possession

Directions: In each sentence cross out any word in the parentheses that does not show possession correctly. Write the correct form in the blank to the right.

Example: My brother seems to have lost (his, h~~i~~'s) pipe. his

1. The loss of a (wife, wife's) income can often add a burden to the family. ____________
2. Some people have no respect for another (person, person's) property. ____________
3. First gather (you, your, you're) equipment before you start baking a cake. ____________
4. A neglected (child, child's) future is very dim. ____________
5. It is sometimes best to let a splinter work (it, its, it's) way out of the finger. ____________
6. John is a good friend of (mine, mines, mine's). ____________
7. My reason for not going is not necessarily the same as (yours, your's). ____________
8. The (fisherman, fisherman's) boat was loaded with tuna. ____________
9. My (teacher, teacher's) pocketbook is on her desk. ____________
10. By fighting the Revolutionary War, the United States won freedom from (it, its, it's) mother country ____________
11. The land was not (our, ours, our's) to trespass on. ____________

12. Parents usually know what's in (their, theirs) children's minds. ________________

5c

***Myself, yourself, himself, herself, itself, ourselves, yourselves,* and *themselves* are never used alone.**

5-9 Using pronouns ending in -self, -selves

Directions: In the following sentences the italicized words either are incorrectly used or misspelled. Write the words that should be substituted for them.

Example: We did all the painting *ourself.* ourselves

1. My sister asks me simple questions she could figure out for *her self.* ________________
2. A man has to condition *hisself* so he will be ready for anything. ________________
3. My brother and *myself* are the laziest people I know. ________________
4. All my classmates and *myself* looked intelligent in our caps and gowns. ________________
5. All the people at the party seemed to be enjoying *theirself.* ________________
6. Did you clean the gutters all by *yourself*? ________________
7. I told my son that I didn't believe the jar had fallen there by *its self.* ________________

5-10 Review

Directions: In the following sentences change any incorrect italicized words and write the correct forms in the blanks to the right. Write *C* in the blank if the italicized word or words are used correctly.

Example: They heard that the money was all *there's.* theirs

1. Soap operas influence *people* attitudes toward love and marriage. ______
2. You nonswimmers would probably like to wet *you* feet. ______
3. Use *Webster New World Dictionary* for definitions. ______
4. That *woman* eyes are brown. ______
5. We saw him talking to his *son's.* ______
6. Leave a note for my husband and *I* if you can't meet us. ______
7. They always know what is happening in *their neighbor's* house. ______
8. Barry *White* voice is deep and masculine. ______
9. *Who's* book do you have? ______
10. Little things often make a *person's* life is better. ______
11. To change a *baby* diaper you should follow certain steps. ______
12. Al couldn't imagine *hisself* playing rock music. ______
13. My sister, my friend, and *myself* walked to school every morning. ______
14. *Its* not going to be an easy test. ______
15. Everything that is *mine* will one day be *yours.* ______
16. Our songs are usually about nature; *their's* are about love. ______

17. I heard *they* voices from the other room. ________________

18. We were told to make *them* beds before the sergeant got here. ________________

19. *Myself and my brother* can do the work of ten men ________________

20. I read the novel from cover to cover, but I couldn't follow *it's* plot. ________________

5-11 Review

Directions: Copy the paragraph below, correcting any errors in the use of pronouns as subjects, objects, and possessive words.

The Rolling Stones gave they're most successful concert of the year at our Civic Center. Mick Jagger, the lead singer, really entertained they audience. Hi's pink satin shirt and green silk pants and silver knee boots impressed my friends and I. Jagger's hair was cut in layers and moved wildly when him and his band danced about the stage. You would have held you breath while he danced nonstop throughout the concert just as I held mines. The other members of the audience were pleased, too, and left the building with smiles on their faces that were just as happy as those that we ourself had on our's.

____

____

____

____

____

____

____

CHAPTER SIX

Agreement

6a
Make each subject agree with its verb.

6-1 Making he, she, it *subjects agree with their verbs*

Directions: In each sentence, cross out the incorrect verb in parentheses. Then write the correct verb in the blank to the right.

Example: A "cool" person (~~know~~, knows) what's happening with the jet set of the town. *knows*

1. She (want, wants) you to have cake and coffee with us after the show. ______
2. My niece always (want, wants) me to buy her things that are too expensive. ______
3. My friend Sandy always (forget, forgets) where she (put, puts) things. ______ ______
4. A slow driver sometimes (cause, causes) an accident just by driving so slowly ______

5. One very seldom (say, says) the word *ridden*, but in writing it's the correct form to use with a helping verb. ______

6-2 Making they *subjects agree with their verbs*

Directions: In each sentence, cross out the incorrect verb in parentheses. Then write the correct verb in the blank to the right.

Example: My pots and pans (look, ~~looks~~) very bad sitting on the stove. look

1. His dimples (show, shows) on both of his cheeks when he smiles. ______
2. My friends usually (laugh, laughs) at my pots because they are old and worn out, but my friends always (want, wants) to use them. ______ ______
3. My closet is filled with lots of things that (get, gets) in my ways. ______
4. Spectators are people that (look, looks) on without taking part. ______
5. The two children (play, plays) together without fighting. ______

6-3 Making he, she, it, *and* they *subjects agree with their verbs*

Directions: In the following sentences, determine which italicized verbs agree with their subjects. Write the correct form of the verb in the blank if the verb is incorrect. Write *C* in the blank to the right if a verb is already correct.

Example: She *goes* to bed late and *sleep* until noon. C
sleeps

1. Diane *sews* most of her clothes, but DeeDee *purchases* ______________

hers. ______________

2. Styling hair *consist* of numerous techniques in arranging

the hair in agreement with one's facial structure. ______________

3. She is a tall, slender lady who *move* gracefully when she ______________

comes on the floor. ______________

4. They are about the same height and *weighs* about the

same. ______________

5. The dynamic wallpaper *make* the room even brighter. ______________

6. Put the equipment back where it *belong.* ______________

7. I like to do most things that *involves* travel. ______________

8. When Friday *comes*, that's when it all *happen.* ______________

____

9. Her personality is just like a magnet that *pull* people to ______________

her and *attract* attention. ______________

10. He *seem* tired today. ______________

6-4 Making **he, she, it,** *and* **they** *subjects agree with their verbs*

Directions: Complete each sentence with the correct present form of the verb or verbs in parentheses.

Example: He always ___takes___ his time. (to take)

1. It is just an empty lot that ______________ back so many memories (to bring).

2. She ______________ very direct when she ______________ to talk.

   (to be, to start)

3. Despite the few problems she ____________ into during the meeting, she ____________ to have everything under control. (to run, to seem)

4. His rounded forehead and bushy eyebrows ____________ him a strange sight to see. (to make)

5. After a while the plants ____________ as if they were growing. (to seem)

6. He has a thin mouth and chin that ____________ molded especially for the rest of his face. (to be)

7. I am not the kind of person who ____________ to go to club meetings. (to like)

8. My best friend ____________ me every night. (to call)

9. Mrs. Hughes ____________ all of her books and ____________ the hospital each morning. (to take, to visit)

10. After she ____________ putting on the makeup, she ____________ her fingernails and ____________ in front of the mirror pretending she is a movie star. (to finish, to polish, to stand)

6-5 *Making* **I, you,** *and* **we** *subjects agree with their verbs*

Directions: In the following sentences, correct the incorrect italicized verbs so that the subjects and verbs agree. Then write the correct verbs in the blanks to the right. Write *C* in the blank if a verb is already correct.

Example: I *teases* him, but he says, "I *know* what I'm doing." tease
C

1. She *fold* her clothes up and *put* them away each evening. ____________
____

2. I *retires* around 11:30 every night. ____________

3. Tom, Andrew, and I *plays* cards most weekends. ______________

4. When I *leaves* the room, the cat jumps onto the couch. ______________

5. Now I *realizes* that I spent too much money on that car. ______________

6. We *knows* we must be in class every day. ______________

7. You can say anything you *wants*, but I still disagree. ______________

8. We always *lose* track of time when we're together, and ______________

   then we *finds* out we're in trouble. ______________

9. She's really a nice person when you *gets* to know her . ______________

10. I *thinks* you *knows* what I *means*. ______________

____

____

6-6 *Making* I, you, *and* we *subjects agree with their verbs*

Directions: Complete the following sentences with the correct present form of the verb or verbs in parentheses

Example: If you ___know___ the other person is wrong, why argue? (to know)

1. You always ______________ you are right. (to think)

2. We usually ______________ to finish our work early. (to try)

3. When I ______________ my baby's smile, I feel happy. (to see)

4. You ______________ impressive when you ______________ a suit. (to look, to wear)

5. I ______________ my son with his homework as much as I can. (to help)

6. My cousin and I ______________ in the church choir together every Sunday. (to sing)

7. You and Sam ___________________ to work harder if you ___________________ to pass this course with the rest of us. (to read, to expect)

8. I ________________ to hurt anyone's feelings, but sometimes I ________________ accidentally. (to mean, to do)

9. Several of my friends and I ___________________ to get the weekend started on Thursday night. (to like)

10. We all ___________________ Lorrie now that she has moved to Florida. (to miss)

6-7 *Using the correct forms of the verb* **be**

Directions: In each sentence, cross out the incorrect verb in parentheses. Then write the correct verb in the blank to the right.

Example: My classmates and I (~~was~~, were) in chorus class going over some songs together. were

1. Her forehead and neck (is, are) smooth and dark. ___________________

2. He fell overboard trying to figure out where the noises (was, were) coming from. ___________________

3. Manners (is, are) important when a child goes to school. ___________________

4. The employment opportunities (was, were) very scarce in the town where I grew up. ___________________

5. It was very hard to study when the house (was, were) ___________________ noisy because the children (was, were) fighting. ___________________

6. Her cheeks (is, are) round and smooth. ___________________

7. The ingredients (is, are) spaghetti, seasoning, and sauce. ___________________

8. Their parrot (is, are) never quiet. ___________________

9. He felt that the animals he hunted (was, were) no match for him. ____________________

10. The best day I had lately (was, were) the day I (was, were) going to the store for my mother and found twenty dollars. ____________________ ____________________

6-8 *Using the correct forms of the verb* be

Directions: Complete the following sentences with the form of the verb *be* that agrees with the subject and fits the time of the sentence (present: *am, is, are* and past: *was, were*).

Example: We got lost and ____were____ unable to find our way home by ourselves.

1. All the people ____________________ looking at me as I got up to give my speech.
2. We passed the written test and ____________________ ready for the road test.
3. My sister and I ____________________ walking home last night when we saw a boy who ____________________ walking six dogs at once.
4. The house ____________________ so dark that I didn't think anyone ____________________ at home until I rang the bell.
5. When Billy came over, Kim and I ____________________ just smiling at each other.
6. There ____________________ four horses in the fields right now.
7. The roads ____________________ really bad that day, and I ____________________ lucky to get there at all.
8. I ____________________ sure that he ____________________ a fair teacher, but he certainly ____________________ hard on us if we don't do our work.

9. Although there __________________ many people who think spending time chasing the ball down the court __________________ crazy, I think basketball __________________ a great game.

10. The music __________________ playing softly, and people __________________ standing around taking and laughing as we come in the door.

6-9 *Using* has *and* have *with the correct subjects*

Directions: In the following sentences, cross out the incorrect italicized verbs and write the correct verbs in the blanks to the right. Write *C* in the blank if the verb is correct.

Example: She *has* a big nose, and her cheeks ~~*has*~~ dark marks on them. ____C____ ____have____

1. Dorothy *have* several children ranging from six to fifteen years old. __________________

2. Nothing *have* changed about my hometown in the last ten years; it still *has* small houses with well-kept lawns and pretty gardens. __________________ __________________

3. Television *have* many bad effects on the family's life style. __________________

4. The beauty is in the historic scenes that the city *have.* __________________

5. When I first moved into my new neighborhood, it was a beautiful and quiet place, but now things *has* changed. __________________

6. After work I am usually tired, so the oldest one of my children *have* to help me make dinner. __________________

7. The park *have* all kinds of rides and a large picnic area. __________________

8. He *have* great legs for running. __________________

9. Because daydreaming is my favorite vice, I never *has* been able to overcome it. ____________________

10. Some classes *have* only a few students in them, but others *has* too many. ____________________ ____________________

6-10 Using **does, goes, do,** *and* **go** *with the correct subjects*

Directions: Complete the following sentences by filling each blank with *does, goes, do,* or *go.*

Example: It ___does___ give me something to hope for when I ___go___ home.

1. I wish someday to be a manager like Mr. Owens, and I hope I understand things the way he ____________________.
2. Mr. Mason is a hard worker and ____________________ all he can for his men.
3. I ____________________ to all the basketball games I can.
4. The thing I like about him is that when he ____________________ something for me, I know he will do a good job.
5. When he is daydreaming, my brother ____________________ not hear a soul.
6. I am the kind of person who ____________________ to all the horror movies that come out.
7. When I ____________________ to my hometown, I always remember the lesson I learned there about not playing tricks on older people.
8. You always ____________________ the best you can for everybody.
9. The color of her hair ____________________ with her complexion perfectly.
10. I like Ken because he is the kind of person who always ____________________ things for other people.

6-11 Using the contractions that agree with their subjects

Directions: In the following sentences, cross out and correct the incorrect italicized contractions so that they agree with their subjects. Write the correct contractions in the blanks to the right. Write *C* in the blank if the contraction is already correct.

Example: Fresh foods ~~*wasn't*~~ as plentiful in Carlson City as they were in Pine View Junction. weren't

1. On the left side of the room there *isn't* any space for the new file cabinets. ______
2. I can remember when there *wasn't* any old buildings or run-down houses in this neighborhood. ______
3. This *don't* give me very much time, and I *don't* like to be late. ______ ______
4. Back in those days, there *wasn't* enough teachers, classrooms, or money for each student to get the right education, but today there *aren't* any excuse for not getting a good education. ______ ______
5. The room *don't* seem too cold now. ______
6. All of the children *hasn't* eaten lunch yet, but they *isn't* hungry yet either. ______ ______
7. Mr. Benson *don't* ever make us eat foods we *don't* like. ______ ______
8. I *hasn't* ever seen him looking like he *hasn't* got a care in the world. ______ ______

9. The streets in this city *wasn't* ever full of potholes, but the streets *wasn't* ever clear of them either. ______ ______

10. My car *don't* start when the weather *isn't* dry. ______ ______

6-12 Using contractions that agree with their subjects

Directions: Complete the following sentences by filling each blank with the contraction *doesn't, don't, wasn't, weren't, isn't, aren't, hasn't,* or *haven't.*

Example: My brother __doesn't__ like to work when he __isn't__ making much money.

1. My new roommate ______ ever on time.
2. My courses ______ seem too difficult as long as I ______ get behind in my work.
3. Some people ______ ever around when you need them, but when you ______ want company, they ______ got sense enough to go home.
4. My little brother ______ much good at housework, but I ______ want to discourage him from helping as long as he ______ keep me from getting my work done.
5. We ______ seen each other in so long that I ______ think we will recognize each other if we ______ both wear red carnations and white sneakers.

6-13 Review

Directions: In the following sentences, correct the incorrect italicized verbs, using present-tense verbs except for *was* and *were.* Write the correct verbs in the blanks to the right. Write *C* in the blank if the verb is correct.

Example: He *has* dreamy eyes that *attract~~s~~* your attention. C

attract

1. Her nose *has* freckles that completely *covers* it.

2. His dedication and devotion *shows* that he *is* a man who *have* a deep sense of responsibility.

3. Just about everybody in this country *own* a TV set or a radio.

4. When the chicken *look* golden brown, it should be done.

5. Diane, who *is* twenty-eight, *has* sparkling brown eyes that *lights* up when she *laugh.*

6.

6. You *can* tell that he's rich by looking at the clothes he *wear.*

7. They *helps* the senior citizens with their meals and also *takes* them to the clinic for their checkups.

8. In the story the main character *swim* to an island and *decide* to hunt for food.

9. The rider *is* judged by the way he *control* his horse.

10. She has eyes that *crinkles* at the edges when she *smile.* ____________

____

11. Remove all the pieces of fabric that *is* left. ____________

12. When I *was* a child riding in the car, I used to make believe that I *were* driving. ____________ ____________

13. Mr. Johnson never *put* any of his employees down or *make* them feel he's better than they are. ____________ ____________

14. There *was* the ferris wheel the octopus, the swings, and many more rides for everyone to enjoy. ____________

15. The hair around his ears *are* gray now. ____________

16. He always *wear* a baseball cap that *sit* on top of his head. ____________

____

17. Al's eyebrows *stand* out from his face but *looks* neatly trimmed. ____________ ____________

18. She's friendly, but she *don't* speak very good English. ____________

19. The red marks on her heavily powdered nose *shows* that she *wears* glasses. ____________ ____________

20. Just the feeling of being out on the lake fishing *make* all the trouble worthwhile. ____________

6-14 Review

Directions: Copy the following paragraph, changing all the italicized verbs from the past tense to the present. Make sure that the present forms of the verbs agree with their subjects. Remember, *will* and *can* go with present tense; *would* and *could* go with past tense.

Jerry *was* the man who *lived* next door to me. He *was* a very quiet man and *seemed* easy-going except when the people in the apartment above his *had* noisy parties on Friday nights. Because I *understood* that these parties *were* just their way of having a good time, I usually *said* nothing when the music *played* loudly and the people *yelled* and *sang.* But Jerry had to get up early because he *worked* Saturdays and *resented* losing his sleep. Each time the noise *got* so loud that the walls *started* to vibrate, Jerry timidly *climbed* the stairs to the second floor, *knocked* on their door, and *requested* that they keep the uproar down a little bit. The neighbors *told* Jerry they *would* and really *meant* to keep their promise, but before Jerry *got* back to sleep the noise *was* pretty loud again. Finally, the party-throwers *found* a solution. They *scheduled* the next party for a Saturday night and *decided* to invite Jerry. Jerry *accepted* the invitation, and on Saturday night he *was* up there with the whole group. He *sang* and *danced* and *ate* and *yelled* as loudly as the rest of them. The next day Jerry *slept* until noon and then *smiled* and *joked* with the party-givers when he *saw* them. He *realized* he *would* have no more trouble sleeping on Friday nights because he was the hit of the party, and they *planned* to have celebrations on Saturdays in the future so they *could* invite him.

6-15 ***Review***

Directions: Complete the following paragraph by filling the blanks with the correct present forms of verbs from the list below. Make sure the verbs agree with their subjects.

dash	drop	stuff	guarantee
watch	be	dream	do (not)
have	go	love	put
come	bring	scream	hope

Basketball ________________ always been my favorite sport. Knowing the stars ________________ from just reading magazines and watching the game. There ________________ nothing more exciting than watching "Dr. J" as he ________________ down the court and ________________ the ball in the basket backward. I ________________ to see the fans that ________________ and ________________ wild, and I ________________ one of them. Then there ________________ "D.T." of the Denver Nuggets, who ________________ ________________ the ball from his hip and ________________ it in the goal. That kind of action ________________ a sellout every night. Sometimes I ________________ that one day I'll be able to dribble like "Earl the Pearl" Monroe, but even if my dreams ________________ come true, basketball will always be my favorite sport.

6b
Make *pronouns* agree with the words they refer to.

NOTE: When a subject could be either male or female, many writers prefer to make the subject plural and to use a plural noun to refer to it.

6-16 Finding the word referred to

Directions: Each of the italicized pronouns in the following sentences refers to a particular word in that sentence. Draw an arrow from the italicized pronoun to the word it refers to. Then write that word in the blank to the right.

Example: The student must bring *his* ticket money. student

1. Each of the boys gets excited about *his* favorite players. ________
2. I thought I had the key to the car, but when we got out of the restaurant, I couldn't find *it*. ________
3. Every now and then she'll find someone who has great talent and present *him* or *her* to a nightclub owner. ________ ________
4. Some courses have only a few students because *they* are not required courses. ________
5. Trust develops when you tell a person something and *she* can keep it to herself. ________
6. I daydream when *my* thoughts wander to some pleasant memory. ________
7. Before petting a strange dog, you should let *it* get used to you. ________
8. Beginning swimmers must first overcome their fear of putting *their* face in water. ________

6-17 *Using the correct singular or plural* pronouns

Directions: Each of the italicized pronouns in the following sentences refers to a particular word in that sentence. Change any italicized pronoun that does not agree with the word it refers to, and write your correction in the blank to the right. If the word is already correct, write *C.* (In some cases, you must also change another word to make it agree with the new pronoun.)

Example: I think there is nothing worse than a person who looks bad in ~~*their*~~ clothes. his or her

1. When a citizen sees a crime being committed, *they* should report it as soon as possible. ________________
2. The word "happiness" is applied when someone is surrounded by loved ones or when *he* is in a peaceful state. ________________
3. A child must be taught to take good care of *their* toys. ________________
4. A firefighter must take many risks with *their* lives to save other people's lives. ________________
5. When a parent refuses to give *their* children something, some children argue in public. ________________
6. If a parent does everything to make children know right from wrong, they will grow up and cause *them* no worry. ________________
7. The students were careful to turn in *their* assignments on time. ________________
8. A good mother is always conscious of *their* children's emotional, as well as physical, needs. ________________
9. The band was ready to begin *its* performance. ________________
10. Inner cities have begun to form communities within *itself.* ________________

6-18 *Choosing the correct singular or plural* **pronouns**

Directions: Change any incorrect italicized pronouns in the following sentences so that they agree with the words they refer to. In some cases you must also change a verb to make it agree with a new pronoun. Write the new paragraph in the space provided.

Example: I dropped my books, and *it* fell in the mud. I dropped my books, and they fell in the mud.

1. Airplanes, automobiles, and trains are three types of modern transportation. *It enables* us to travel much more than people could in the past. *He* used to have to walk or use horses to get from place to place, but now, by using cars and planes, people can have breakfast in New York City and dinner in London. We cannot always depend on these means of transportation to get us everywhere, but *it* can shorten the distances between cities, states, and even countries.

2. Because dogs were companionable and intelligent, people put *it* to work very early in history. Stone Age caves picture people and dogs together on what seem to be hunting

expeditions. People probably bred and trained dogs to hunt for food and trained the dogs to protect *him* from wild animals. ________________________________

3. Ten or fifteen years ago most of the mechanics did not have a high-school education or school training. Many of *them* learned *his* skills on farm tractors or in *their* fathers' garages. I think that *they* were the best because *he* knew how to do the job and *he* didn't mind taking the responsibility of *their* job. ________________________________

4. Visiting nurses are public health nurses. So are the nurses employed by city, county, or state health departments. The public health nurses may go into homes to care for *their* patients who have just returned from hospitals. *She* often *teaches* patients and

their families about proper diet. *She* may also teach *him* about personal cleanliness and ways of preventing illness. The reward for nurses is most often the knowledge that *her* skill has helped to relieve suffering. ______________________

5. The successful student comes to class well prepared and on time. *They* have *their* books and assignments with *them*, and before class begins this type of student makes sure that *his* pencils are sharp and that *he* has paper and several pens. *They* usually sit in the front of the room, and if *they* must miss class, the good student has a friend tell *him* what went on in class and take notes for *them* so that *their* work will not be turned in late. This type of student often gets high grades, and *they* always have the satisfaction of knowing that *they* have made a sincere effort to learn. ______________

____

____

____

____

____

____

____

6-19 Choosing the correct singular or plural form

Directions: In the following sentences, cross out the incorrect pronoun in parentheses. Then write the correct pronoun in the blank to the right.

Example: The students brought (~~his~~, their) pets to school. their

1. The children insisted on doing it (himself, themselves). ____________
2. Someone forgot (his, their) ticket to the play. ____________
3. I bought new eyeglasses, and (it, they) really make me look different. ____________
4. He bought new slacks, but (it, they) had to be returned because of a tear in a seam. ____________
5. A nurse is known for (her, their) dedication. ____________
6. The average mother wants (her, their) children to grow up to be pleasant and helpful adults. ____________
7. If each does (his, their) best, (he, they) will get the job ____________ done on time. ____________
8. Americans today want to work to make this a better

country for (himself, themselves) and (his, their) children ________________

to live in. ________________

9. Horses are complex animals. (It is, They are) popular with many young people today. Learning to ride (it, them) is ________________

also a challenge. ________________

10. Men want (his, their) children to get to know (him, them). ________________

In addition (they also want, he also wants) more time to ________________

spend with (his, their) families. ________________

____

6-20 Choosing the correct pronoun: **his, her,** *or* **their**

Directions: In each of the following sentences, decide whether *his, her,* or *their* should go in the blank. Then write your answer. (In some cases either *his* or *her* may be used.)

Example: Each person should bring ___*his*___ money to school.

1. Everyone should do ________________ own work.
2. A student who works hard will probably get good grades on ________________ report card.
3. Neither brother remembered ________________ money.
4. Either Ned or Mark will bring ________________ frisbee.
5. One of the children lost ________________ lunch money.
6. Neither John nor Allen ever studies ________________ math.
7. One of the club members raised ________________ hand.
8. Both boys liked ________________ day at the beach.
9. Each of the children missed ________________ bus.

10. Larry and Tom left ____________________ jackets at school.

11. All of the members paid ____________________ dues.

12. Someone must have left ____________________ wallet on the chair.

6-21 Choosing the correct singular or plural **pronoun**

Directions: In the following sentences, some of the italicized pronouns are correct and some are incorrect. If a pronoun is incorrect, cross it out and write the correct pronoun in the blank to the right. If a pronoun is correct, put *C* in the blank. (In some cases either *his* or *her* may be used.)

Example: One of the boys got an A on *his* paper. ______C______

1. Because a theater seat is used so much, *they* get worn-looking quickly. ____________________
2. Everything is in *its* place. ____________________
3. Each bird fought hard for *their* share of food. ____________________
4. I eat many fruits because *it is* good for me. ____________________
5. Someone keeps mumbling under *his* breath. ____________________
6. I sold my painting for more than *they were* worth. ____________________
7. I like modern kinds of art because *they express* a great deal of feeling. ____________________
8. Each of the children washed *their* hands before dinner. ____________________
9. One of my kittens *has* stripes on *their* back. ____________________

    ____
10. I forgot something. Will you get *it* for me? ____________________
11. Each of the ladies brought *their* umbrella. ____________________
12. *He* is the kind of friend you can depend on. ____________________

CHAPTER SEVEN

Verbs

7a

Learn the verb forms that express the past.

7-1 Using simple past forms ending in **-ed**

Directions: If any of the following sentences shows that something happened in the past, make the italicized verb past by rewriting the word (adding *-d* or *-ed*). If you cannot tell whether past or present is intended, do not change the verb or write anything in the blank.

Example: Yesterday I *change*d a tire on my sister's car. changed

1. My father *accomplish* a great deal during his school days. ____________

2. We get together and talk about all the things we *use* to do as children. ____________

3. I really *enjoy* high school for several reasons. ____________

4. My accident last summer severely *damage* my car. ____________

7-2 Using simple past forms ending in **-ed**

Directions: Edit the following paragraph, correcting all errors in the use of past (*-ed*) endings. Circle each verb error, and write your correction above it.

I use to spend every Saturday drag racing my motorcycle, so it was important to me to maintain my equipment properly. First I needed to take care of the protective gear that I wore. This gear consist of a helmet, a thick leather coat, a pair of leather pants, gloves, and boots with metal toes. I always carried a tool kit. This kit had an assortment of wrenches that allow me to make minor repairs. Spare tires and extra gasoline were a must if I wanted to race more than once. I had an extra engine that I turn to only if the other engine seem beyond repair. Finally I had a pickup truck in which I haul everything up to the track. The equipment was important because it help to keep me in the race.

7-3 Using irregular past forms

Directions: Some of the following sentences show that something happened in the past. Some of them show action in the present. In each sentence cross out the incorrect verb in parentheses. Then write the correct word in the blank to the right.

Example: My heart (~~sink~~, sank) when the teacher asked that questions. *sank*

1. The struggle for equal employment opportunities (begin, began) many years ago. ______
2. While I was on vacation, my money (run, ran) out. ______
3. Every day last semester I (sing, sang) on my way to school. ______
4. The *Titanic*'s passengers (sing, sang) as the ship (sink, sank). ______ ______
5. During her childhood Tina always (drink, drank) her milk eagerly. ______
6. The birds (sing, sang) constantly outside my window while I was sick last summer. ______

7. (Drink, Drank) at least six glasses of water daily. ________

8. My fish hooks (sink, sank) into the water as soon as I throw them in. ________

9. Pepper, my dog, (run, ran) out to meet me when I got off the bus. ________

10. Before you (begin, began) your work, turn off the television. ________

7-4 Using **blew, drew, flew, grew,** *and* **knew**

Directions: If the italicized verb in each of the following sentences expresses the past correctly, write *C* in the blank at the right. If the verb is not correct, change it. Then write the correct form.

Example: Just as the firefighters reached the burning house, its roof *blowed* off. blew

1. Last year the demand for pet food *grew* even though its price increased. ________

2. John, a true fan of boxing, thought he *knowed* more than the referee. ________

3. Upon entering the holding pattern, the aircraft *flew* directly to an assigned altitude. ________

4. The wind *blew* so fiercely during the storm that our mobile home shook. ________

5. In art class all the beginners *drawed* a vase of flowers. ________

6. Mac's kite *flied* so high we could hardly see it. ________

7. Thinking she *knew* enough about sewing, my friend Pamela dropped the course. __________

8. I covered my hair with a kerchief because the wind *blowed* it all over my face. __________

9. My grandfather *drawed* up his chair and started to tell the story again. __________

10. Enrollment in community colleges *growed* rapidly from 1970 to 1975. __________

7-5 *Using* swore, tore, *and* wore

Directions: When the past is needed in the following sentences, change the italicized verb to *swore, tore,* or *wore.* Then write the correct verb in the blank to the right. Write *C* if the sentence is already correct.

Example: Every day last spring I ~~*wear*~~ the same old coat to school. wore

1. When she tried to crawl through the fence, Eloise *tear* her dress. __________

2. Pete leaned so hard on his pencil that he *weared* down the point. __________

3. Although he *swore* to tell the truth, Alvin withheld some evidence from the court. __________

4. When I got married, the bridal party all *wear* formal clothes. __________

5. In his anger he *teared* the paper into many small pieces. __________

6. My son was accused of stealing that book, but he *sweared* he didn't do it. __________

7-6 *Using* came *and* became

Directions: If the italicized verb in each of the following sentences expresses the past correctly, write *C* in the blank to the right. If the verb is not correct, change it. Then write the correct form of the verb in the blank.

Example: I *became* afraid of electrical storms as I grew older. C

1. Al *come* to understand his mother and father only after he left home. ________
2. I have often wondered what *become* of my high-school friends. ________
3. Last year the whole family *came* to our house for Christmas dinner. ________
4. Once Jim *become* angry, he didn't listen to one word I said. ________
5. All of a sudden the right answer *come* to me. ________

7-7 *Using* did, saw, *and other irregular verb forms*

Directions: Some of the following sentences show that something happened in the past. Some of them show action in the present. In each sentence cross out the incorrect word in parentheses. Then write the correct word in the blank to the right.

Example: Students who (~~go~~, went) on the trip were excused earlier. went

1. We always (shake, shook) out the rugs before we dust the furniture. ________
2. The fact that you (forget, forgot) my birthday made me sad. ________
3. Who (give, gave) you the money to go to last week's dance? ________

4. I (seen, saw) you take the last piece of cake at lunch. ____________________

5. Steve (eat, ate) so much I'm surprised that he didn't get sick. ____________________

6. Those boys (did, done) some things they were sorry for. ____________________

7. I always (take, took) a book when I go to the beach. ____________________

8. My mother (fell, fall) last winter and broke her hip. ____________________

9. When you (go, went) to the store this morning, did you notice the price of milk? ____________________

10. Tom believed that he had passed the course only after he (saw, seen) his report card. ____________________

7-8 Using irregular past forms

Directions: In the blank provided, write the past form of each verb in parentheses.

Example: Last week someone ___broke___ into my car. (break)

1. Our gardenia plant ____________________ because we forgot to cover it carefully last winter. (freeze)
2. My father ____________________ to Washington last Sunday. (drive)
3. We all ____________________ to the picnic in the back of Dan's truck. (ride)
4. The teacher ____________________ briefly before passing out the papers. (speak)
5. Whenever any problems ____________________, we always asked Maria to solve them. (arise)
6. Bob ____________________ his theme very carefully. (write)
7. Because I decided to use the clothes dryer, the sun ____________________ all day. (shine)

8. The track team ____________________ our school's long-standing record for relay racing. (break)

9. Whoever ____________________ the library books should return them immediately. (steal)

10. Harry ____________________ to join the Navy in order to see the world. (choose)

7-9 *Using* burst, caught, dug, led, *and* passed

Directions: If the verbs in each of the following sentences express the past correctly, write *C* in the blank to the right. If any verb is not correct, change it. Then write the correct form in the blank.

Example: My dog di~~gg~~ed in my father's garden. ___dug___

1. The firefighters led three frightened people from the burning house. ____________________
2. Alvin catched five crabs in his crab trap. ____________________
3. I finally past my chemistry course. ____________________
4. John continued to blow up the balloon until it finally busted. ____________________
5. The cheerleaders leaded the football players onto the field. ____________________
6. Time passed quickly in that interesting class. ____________________
7. The land crabs dug tiny holes in the sand. ____________________
8. While I was canning the beans, one of the jars busted. ____________________
9. Tom caught the ball easily. ____________________
10. The exploding dynamite digged an enormous hole in the field. ____________________

7-10 Review

Directions: In the following sentences cross out the incorrect forms of the verb in parentheses and write the correct forms in the blanks to the right.

Example: One spring day in 1977 I (p~~lant~~t, planted) a garden. planted

1. Every spring when the season opens, I (get, got) the urge to go fishing. ____________________
2. As time went by and I anxiously (await, awaited) my transfer date, I (gather, gathered) more information about my new school. ____________________ ____________________
3. Finally the great day (arrived, arrive) and I left my ship. ____________________
4. We (begin, began) our homework after that TV program ended. ____________________
5. Now Peter and Sue always (run, ran) home from the school bus stop. ____________________
6. They (drink, drank) their coffee slowly as they discussed the day's events. ____________________
7. Pollen (flies, flew) through the air when the wind blows. ____________________
8. When I was younger, I thought I (knew, knowed) everything. ____________________
9. During yesterday's severe storm several small boats (sink, sank). ____________________
10. Megan (drawed, drew) a picture of a Halloween pumpkin. ____________________
11. She (tears, tore) her dress when she fell off the curb. ____________________

12. When I (become, became) tired, I am unable to keep up with the other swimmers. ________

13. Every member of the team (done, did) his best to win the game. ________

14. Every time he (saw, seen) me, he always smiled and spoke. ________

15. Several of my friends (come, came) to our house last night. ________

7-11 Review

Directions: Copy each of the following sentences, changing the verb to the past tense. Underline the verbs that you change.

Example: That fabric shrinks easily. That fabric shrank easily.

1. He wears a clean shirt every day. ________

2. We play cards every Saturday night. ________

3. Many joggers run at least three miles a day. ________

4. The strong wind shakes the petals from the flowers. ________

5. After working for a while, people often come to realize the importance of education. ________

6. That glass breaks easily. ________

7. Bridges freeze earlier than the rest of the highway. ______________________

____

8. I choose you as my partner. ______________________________

____

9. Paul writes to his mother very often. ______________________

____

10. Everyone rides to school on the bus. ______________________

____

11. Most students want good marks in their classes. ______________

____

12. He drives recklessly despite my warning. ____________________

____

13. After dinner I begin the day's assignments. __________________

____

14. Dead limbs and branches fall from the trees. _________________

____

15. Michael always gives his brother financial help. ______________

____

16. He goes that way often. ________________________________

____

17. We use our own notebook paper in class. ____________________

____

18. My baby grows so quickly! ______________________________

____

19. Sometimes Sally forgets to telephone her mother. ____________________

____

20. Usually, someone in class knows the right answer to all the instructor's questions.

____

____

7b
Learn to use regular and irregular past participles.

7-12 Using regular past participles

Directions: Edit the following paragraph, correcting all errors in the use of *-ed* endings. Circle each verb error, and write your correction above it.

My dishes are always wash in an orderly way. First, all the dishes are place close to the sink. Then I run water into the sink and pour dishwashing detergent into the water. When the sink is fill with warm, sudsy water, the glasses are place in the water alone. When the glasses seem free of dirt, I rinse them in clean water and place them in a dish drain. Next, the plates are wash in the same way. Then the silverware is placed into the sink and each piece is washed separately. Finally, the pots and pans are scrub one at a time. At last, the job of washing dishes is finish.

7-13 Using regular past participles

Directions: Some of the following sentences contain an incorrect verb form. Circle the incorrect form and rewrite it correctly in the blank to the right. If the sentence is already correct, write *C* in the blank.

Examples: She has never (listen) to good advice. listened

By eleven-thirty he had danced for three hours. C

1. He has use my car so often that I am tired of lending it to him. ____________

2. The new law is suppose to help old or handicapped people keep their homes. ____________

3. My friend has envy me ever since I bought some new clothes. ____________

4. By the time I am finished with my sewing, I am happy again. ____________

5. Be sure that you have clean all of the cabinets and counters. ____________

6. I know a girl who has receive trophies and a scholarship because she is a good runner. ____________

7. Are twins suppose to dress alike all the time? ____________

8. We moved to the circulation desk, where books are checked out and return. ____________

9. Teenagers are frequently influenced by movies and television. ____________

10. After owning one for two years, I have experience many problems with that make of car. ____________

7-14 Using irregular past participles

Directions: In the following sentences circle any verb form that needs to be changed. Then write the correct form in the blank to the right. If a sentence is correct, write *C* in the blank.

Examples: Can't you tell that she has never (sing) that number before? sung

The snow had begun to fall faster. C

1. My new jeans have shrank so much that I can't wear them. ______

2. Many people have run the famous Boston Marathon. ______

3. Before I knew what was going on, she had begin to give my lunch to her dog. ______

4. He wrecked his car after he had drank too much of Mr. Brownley's wine. ______

5. The pipe has sprung a leak, and I can't find a plumber. ______

6. The choir had always sang such beautiful songs that I couldn't believe they sounded so terrible. ______

7. Have you began your typing classes this semester? ______

8. The councilmen have ran up the city's expenses to the danger point. ______

9. The bad storm has flooded some streets and has sank many small boats. ______

10. Have you ever drank fresh pineapple juice? ______

7-15 Using irregular past participles

Directions: A verb is given in parentheses after each of the following sentences. Write the correct form of that verb in the blank space in the sentence.

Example: The protestors have torn down signs and trampled the shrubbery. (tear)

1. The problem could be that this person has just ____________________ up on life. (give)

2. He has ____________________ everything you cank think of. (steal)

3. Some politicians have ____________________ votes and then forgotten the people who elected them. (take)

4. Be sure that the emblem is ____________________ on the left sleeve of the jacket. (wear)

5. Because of fear, no one has ____________________ against the proposal. (speak)

6. They were ____________________ to take action because their neighbors would do nothing. (drive)

7. This plan is ____________________ to be one way out of a difficult situation. (see)

8. Last night's wind was so violent that many of the young trees were ____________________. (break)

9. In spite of bad publicity many people have ____________________ here every day. (eat)

10. After reading the article, he had ____________________ a critical letter to the author. (write)

7-16 Using irregular past participles

Directions: In the following sentences circle any verb form that needs to be changed. Then write the correct form in the blank to the right. If a sentence is correct, write *C*.

Examples: The wind has (blowed) hard all day. ____blown____

Have you ever flown in a jet plane? ____C____

1. The bushes have growed until the house is out of sight. ____________________

2. No contractor could build anything from the plans that this man has drew. ____________

3. After coming for food every day during the winter, the birds have now flyed away north. ____________

4. The child has finally grown tall enough to wear the beautiful dress her grandmother made for her. ____________

5. The explosion had blowed out windows for three or four blocks around it. ____________

6. The model homes were then shown to prospective buyers. ____________

7. Those poor people have never knowed any other way of life. ____________

8. The whole town was alarmed when the material for the new school was showed to be faulty and even dangerous. ____________

9. A circle was drawn around each problem that had an error in it. ____________

10. Has the pilot ever flew that type of plane before today? ____________

7-17 Using gone, done, come, *and* become

Directions: In each of the following sentences one of the above verbs has been used incorrectly. Circle the incorrect form; then write the correct form in the blank to the right. After making the correction, write a sentence of your own, using a helping verb and the verb given in parentheses.

Example: Spring had (came) early that year. *come*

(come) *The packages that we were waiting for have finally come.*

1. I thought she was my friend, but she has did nothing to help me when I needed it. ________

(done) ________

2. The issue has became very important in the current election. ________

(become) ________

3. They had never came here before this year. ________

(come) ________

4. Unless you want to buy new tires right away, rotate them before the wear has went any further. ________

(gone) ________

7-18 Using gone, done, come, *and* become

Directions: If the wrong form of *gone, done, come,* or *become* has been used in any of the following sentences, circle the wrong word and then write the correct form in the blank to the right. If the sentence is correct, write *C* in the blank.

Examples: She has never (came) to a class on time. come

What have you done with the test papers? C

When she came in, she wouldn't speak to anyone. C

1. Our neighbor's dog has did a great deal of damage to our little garden. ________

2. Has the class gone over the last problem yet? ____________

3. Belinda has never became friendly with the other girls in the office. ____________

4. After she had did her typing, Louise picked up a book and began to read. ____________

5. The movie, according to the newspapers, became a new box-office hit. ____________

6. I think I recognize those people who have came to see my sister. ____________

7. After the crowd had gone away, Rennie went back to find ____________ out what had been done with the flags and banners. ____________

8. Home computers have became necessities in many American homes. ____________ ____________

9. Although they have went, they have not been forgotten. ____________

10. Haven't you come to the exciting part of the story yet? ____________

7-19 Review of irregular verbs

Directions: A verb is given in parentheses after each of these sentences. Write the correct form of that verb in the blank space in the sentence.

Example: The city has just ___dug___ a big hole in our yard. (dig)

1. Most of his time is ____________ doing small things around the kitchen. (spend)

2. I have never ____________ a large fish. (catch)

3. That woman ____________ all of her children and grandchildren to stay at our house for a week. (bring)

4. Many people have ____________________ by without seeing it. (pass)

5. If it has ____________________, the main water valve must be turned off right away. (burst)

6. They were very annoyed to find that the dog had ____________________ up all the flowers. (dig)

7. When the resolution was ____________________, everyone cheered and applauded. (pass)

8. The members of the family fought and fussed until their grandfather's will was ____________________. (find)

9. Since Ron ____________________ his ankle, you will run in the relays tomorrow. (hurt)

10. The dog was ____________________ to bring the cows and sheep in from the pasture each evening. (teach)

7-20 Review of past participles

Directions: Circle any verb form below that needs to be changed. Then write the correct form in the blank to the right. If more than one form in a sentence is incorrect, make all necessary changes. If the sentence is already correct, write *C* in the blank.

Examples: If Flora has (learn) the routine, tell her she has (became) the leader for the drill team. ____learned____ ____become____

The news report said that all of the people had reached shelter in time. ____C____

1. As you can see, the idea has been express in several ways. ____________________

2. Just knowing that you have help someone else can be very rewarding. ____________________

3. After he had ran for five minutes, Bernie knew that he must go faster or lose the cross-country race. ____________

4. They had never drank anything so delicious, and most of the group asked for more. ____________

5. Several judges have wrote papers about the unpopular decision. ____________

6. Everyone I knew had moved away from that area of town, ____________ and many stores had been build there. ____________

7. To their surprise, no one had took the boxes and the large suitcase. ____________

8. The boys didn't try to go because the accident had done so much damage to their car. ____________

9. Before I knew it, my name was call. ____________

10. The students came running in after the bus had went. ____________

11. Of all the things I have losed in my life, I think I miss my little gold bracelet the most. ____________

12. I don't know why Marie has became so hostile; after all, ____________ it isn't my fault that Ricky has decide that he likes me. ____________

13. The mountains are very beautiful since spring has came. ____________

14. I didn't recognize my brother-in-law because he had grew ____________ a large mustache since I had last see him. ____________

15. Everyone in the class laughed when they saw they had all bought notebooks of the same color. ____________

7c

Add the present participle (*-ing*) ending to a verb that tells that something is continuing.

7-21 Using -ing *verbs correctly*

Directions: In each of the following sentences cross out the incorrect word in parentheses. Then write the correct word in the blank to the right.

Example: Did you say the boys are (~~run~~, running) in the race right now? *running*

1. They were (drive, driving) to work when the accident happened. ______
2. While she was (walk, walking) down the street a man ran out and grabbed her purse. ______
3. She always (talks, talking) about the good old days. ______
4. Technicians are now (find, finding) several reasons for the problems with the machine. ______
5. The mayor will (go, going) to every civic organization meeting next week. ______
6. He was (speak, speaking) to the class when you called, and I gave him your message when he finished. ______
7. Listen for knocks and strange noises when the motor is (ran, running). ______
8. They were (watch, watching) TV when the electric current went off. ______
9. Several pickets were (march, marching) up and down in front of the store when I went in. ______

7d
Learn to use the verb *be* correctly.

7-22 *Using forms of the verb* be

Directions: In each of the following sentences cross out any incorrect form of the verb *be* that you find in parentheses. Then write the correct form of *be* in the blank to the right.

Example: This town doesn't look like the place where I (was, ~~been~~) born and raised. ___was___

1. Did you forget that a man (was, were) going to call you at six? ______
2. My friends will (be, been) here at noon. ______
3. On Saturdays I (am, be) dusting the living room whenever you look for me. ______
4. Pick up those papers; they (being, are being) scattered all over the room. ______
5. My friend Ronald (been, has been) good to me. ______
6. If I (was, were) you, I wouldn't take so many naps. ______
7. Because I (am, be) now attending the community college in this area, I can easily come in for a job interview. ______
8. Edna (been, has been) spoiling those children for a long time. ______
9. Sometimes I think you (being, are being) stubborn. ______
10. When I walk into the noisy dining room, sound (be, is) vibrating from the walls. ______

11. We (been, have been) friends for a long time now. ____________

7-23 Using forms of the verb **be**

Directions: Make a caret (∧) to show where *is, are, was, were, has,* or *have* should be inserted in each of the following sentences. Then write the word to be inserted.

Example: Although I try, it ∧ sometimes difficult to be an understanding person. *is*

1. As the story opens, Rainsford sailing on a yacht with his friend Whitney. ____________
2. I think husbands and wives should always look good for one another, no matter how long they been married. ____________
3. His hair cut neatly, and he was cleanly shaven. ____________
4. Everyone waiting yesterday for the bus to Hoboken. ____________
5. California a place I have always wanted to visit. ____________
6. We been waiting for a long time for one of those apartments. ____________
7. We grew up together, so we always been close. ____________
8. In my hometown so many things being changed for the better. ____________
9. Everyone at the Recreation Center been playing pool, watching a movie, or just talking. ____________

7e

Change the form of a verb only when necessary.

7-24 Using helpers that change verbs and helpers that don't

Directions: In each sentence below cross out the incorrect helper in parentheses. Then write the correct helper in the blank to the right.

Example: I (will, ~~have~~) visit my sister in Hawaii soon. will

1. Our neighbors (may, have) call on us at any time. ______
2. If Annie (had, did) exercised more, she would not (have, ______ had) needed to watch her weight. ______
3. These are some of the students who (have, could) already graduated. ______
4. It is clear that Ed (should, has) decided what to do. ______
5. Do you think it (is, might) rain today? ______
6. He (can't, hasn't) listened to a word you've said. ______
7. If my brother (didn't, wasn't) cooperate with you, then ______ you (haven't, can't) changed his point of view. ______
8. Harry certainly could have (finished, finish) those math problems if he had tried. ______
9. My cousins in North Carolina (would, have) often stayed out in the sun too long on nice beach days. ______
10. It seems that no one (has, should) answered the letter. ______

7-25 *Using helpers that change verbs and helpers that don't*

Directions: Complete the following sentences by inserting your own verb in each blank.

Example: You can always ___succeed___ if you really try.

1. I know I should __________, but I can't always do it.
2. The mechanic can easily __________ the job by next Tuesday.
3. By the time you call, we will __________ what to do.
4. Last week my sister did __________ a letter from her friend in New York.
5. Don't __________ an exit; stay right on that road.
6. On the left you will __________ a sign saying St. Paul's Boulevard.
7. A person can __________ different accessories to go with each outfit.
8. If you don't mention it, he won't ever __________ the difference.
9. If I studied harder, I would __________ better grades.
10. I didn't __________ that those papers were still on the desk.

7f
Use the correct forms of *lay* and *lie*, and *set* and *sit*.

7-26 *Using the correct forms of* lay *and* lie

Directions: Write *lay, lie, laid, laying,* or *lying* in the blank provided in each of the following sentences.

Example: ___Lie___ still.

1. Yesterday I __________ on the beach all day.
2. The oysters were __________ on the plate.
3. Esther __________ her packages down carefully.

4. Have you had any experience in ____________________ bricks?

5. This is a good day to ____________________ around without doing anything.

6. ____________________ in bed for a few minutes after awakening will help a person begin a good day.

7-27 Using the correct forms of **set** *and* **sit**

Directions: Write *set, sit, sat, sitting,* or *setting* in the blank provided in each of the following sentences.

Example: Joe ____sat____ quietly in his chair.

1. ____________________ down, and don't say a word.

2. My father ____________________ out the tomato plants in neat rows.

3. Is that your aunt ____________________ with your mother on the front porch?

4. I was afraid to speak, so I just ____________________ and waited.

5. Are you ____________________ aside several minutes a day for reading and thinking?

7-28 Using **lay** *and* **lie***;* **set** *and* **sit**

Directions: In each sentence below cross out the incorrect form in parentheses. Then write the correct word in the blank to the right.

Example: His long, neat blond hair (~~lays~~, lies) on his shoulders. ____lies____

1. He went straight to the table where the food was (laying, lying). ____________________

2. The house (set, sat) on a high bluff. ____________________

3. I got tired of seeing those clothes (laying, lying) around. ____________________

4. In my dining room there is a long black chair that I (set, sit) in every day. ____________________

5. (Set, Sit) your board up straight, and then drive a nail through it. ____________

6. I can talk on the phone and be (laying, lying) down and resting at the same time. ____________

7. When my brother comes home from school, he first gets something to eat and then (lays, lies) around watching TV until supper time. ____________

8. One day I (set, sat) myself down and made up my mind to stop smoking. ____________

9. Many people enjoy hiking, swimming, and just plain (laying, lying) around. ____________

10. Most of the time my cat (lays, lies) where it can be seen. ____________

7g
Use verbs to help you tell time.

7-29 Telling whether time is past, present, or future

Directions: In each sentence below decide whether the time is past, present, or future. Then cross out the incorrect form of the verb in parentheses and write the correct form in the blank to the right.

Example: Although my father is stern, all of us (respect, ~~respected~~) him. *respect*

1. People in my country could afford luxuries only if they (belong, belonged) to a well-to-do family. ____________

2. They say it's bad luck if you (try, tried) on your wedding dress before your wedding. ____________

3. After you (warm, warmed) the house, fill up the tub. ____________

4. Sam always comes into the classroom, (takes, took) a seat, and then doesn't say anything. ____________

5. I felt his forehead to see if he (has, had) a fever. ____________

6. After a man gained the respect of a woman's family, he (can, could) then ask for her hand in marriage. ____________

7. Receiving a gift from my brother was a surprise because I (haven't, hadn't) heard from him in months. ____________

8. At first I thought it (was, is) fun to have snow, but when it comes, it causes many difficulties. ____________

9. When I returned to my old neighborhood amusement center, I felt bad about the way the children (abused, had abused) it over the years. ____________

10. It was fall when we moved here, and the weather (is, was) pleasant until the temperature got down to the freezing point. ____________

7-30 Using **would** *in telling time*

Directions: In each sentence below the italicized verb form is incorrect. Cross it out and write the correct verb form in the space provided to the right.

Examples: If you ~~*would scrape*~~ the food from the dishes, it would be easier to wash them. scraped

If the doctor ~~*would have arrived*~~ a little later, my sister would have developed blood poisoning. had arrived

1. If you walk into a bar these days, you *would see* as many women as men. ______________

2. Our society would benefit if people *would relax* a little more. ______________

3. If you have your own house, you *would find* that utilities cost around $100 a month. ______________

4. Each time I *will stop* for a red light, the motor would die. ______________

5. You should scrape the food from the dishes so the dish-water *would be* cleaner. ______________

6. If you follow these steps carefully, you *would have* very few problems. ______________

7. Sometimes I wished that some of my classmates *would have gone* to someone else for help. ______________

8. If you *would have washed* your pots last, I would not have broken any of your dishes. ______________

9. If a person *would buy* an old car now, it would cost a lot of money. ______________

10. When she returns home from work, she *would change* clothes, fix dinner, and relax. ______________

11. If a driver will slow down and watch himself carefully, many accidents *wouldn't happen.* ______________

12. Every time I *tell* Joe to stop eating so much, he would look at me and keep right on eating. ____________

7-31 *Using* **would** *in telling time*

Directions: Complete each of the following sentences. Use *would* in the part you add.

Example: If I had only known the truth, I would have warned him.

1. If you had made the bed properly, ____________
2. If they went to her wedding, ____________
3. If we were willing to listen, ____________
4. If I had stayed at home and studied for that exam, ____________
5. If your sister had been driving the car, ____________

7-32 *Using* **would** *in telling time*

Directions: Complete each of the following sentences.

Example: I would have wanted to be at that performance if it had been possible.

1. Sally would have been eager to ____________
2. Would you have been too frightened to ____________
3. If my parents had known, they would have asked me to ____________
4. If you had written, I would have rushed to ____________

5. Under the circumstances, Edith and I would not have been able to ______________

____

7-33 Using **would** *and* **will** *in telling time*

Directions: Fill in *would* or *will* to complete each of the following sentences.

Example: After I receive your letter, I ___will___ send you a reply.

1. I am sure that I ______________ be ready by seven.
2. Even if we changed our clothes, we ______________ still have time for a walk.
3. Mr. Moore found that he ______________ need several more ten-penny nails to repair the barn door.
4. I know that I ______________ hear something soon.
5. If my father hadn't been drafted, he ______________ never have had the chance to visit Germany.
6. As usual, our ducks decided that they ______________ wait at the back door for a handout.
7. I wonder what I ______________ take to the cookout.
8. I ______________ definitely be outside the theater when the doors open.
9. When Eric gives you his opinion, ______________ you trust his judgment?
10. When summer came, we ______________ always go to visit my grandmother.

7h
Recognize words that only look like verbs.

7-34 Recognizing words that look like verbs

Directions: If the italicized word or words in any of these sentences are used as verbs, write *V*. If the italicized words are not used as verbs, write the verb or verbs used in the sentence.

Examples: She was *laughing* hysterically. ____V____

Laughing hysterically, my sister got up and ran out of the room. ____got up, ran____

1. *Working* out in the gym proved difficult by rewarding. ________
2. To *estimate* the cost, you should refer to last year's price list. ________
3. There is a sign in the library that says "No *Talking.*" ________
4. To *be* certain of getting to the movie on time, leave your home early. ________
5. She *was* still *wondering* how she would find the letter. ________
6. Sometimes it becomes necessary to listen patiently to her endless stories without *saying* a word. ________
7. To *calculate* income tax without having to pay an accountant, a person needs a certain amount of experience. ________
8. *Whispering* in my brother's ear that I wanted to talk with him, I looked toward the door. ________
9. Try to *listen.* ________
10. I *am telling* everyone here the news before a formal announcement is made. ________

7-35 Using **-ing** *words and* **infinitives**

Directions: Cross out the incorrect form in parentheses; then write the correct form in the blank to the right.

Example: Place the dishes in the order in which you want to (wash, ~~washed~~) them. wash

1. Spray your furniture and watch it (shine, shines) like a mirror. ____________
2. (Trade, Trading) cars is an expensive practice. ____________
3. (Grab, Grabbing) his hat, Mr. Askew started out the door. ____________
4. The new houses make the whole community (look, looks) new. ____________
5. By about noon the clouds began to (roll, rolled) in from the north end of the beach. ____________
6. Sometimes we have to (give, gives) up some of the things we want to do. ____________
7. He used after-shave lotion to (attract, attracted) the attention of the ladies. ____________
8. The repairs to the community center really helped to (improve, improved) the place. ____________
9. I was (walk, walking) through the shipyard on my way to work when I witnessed an accident. ____________
10. I can hardly wait for the fishing season to (start, started). ____________

7-36 Using -ing words as verbs, nouns, and adjectives

Directions: Write *V, N,* or *A* to show whether the italicized word or expression in each sentence below is used as a verb, a noun, or an adjective.

Example: *Canoeing* is fun. ____N____

1. After I had tried to drive to California a few times, *flying* began to seem like a good idea. ________
2. *Smiling* to myself, I told my brother the answer. ________
3. Ivan was *standing* in front of Rainsford. ________
4. A person should do some careful *thinking* before deciding to act. ________
5. Someone *hoping* to be a really good billiard player needs a steady hand and good judgment. ________

CHAPTER EIGHT

Making Sense of Sentences

8a
Avoid the mixed-up sentence.

8-1 Avoiding the **in which, for which, of which** *trap*

Directions: Correct any mixed-up sentence by crossing out *in, for, of,* or *to* when it is not necessary to the meaning of the sentence.

Example: The tour guides were surprised to find out they would have to pay for the uniforms ~~in~~ which they wear.

1. The other section of the store in which is hard for people to resist is the food department.
2. For this sport a person uses a surfboard with a cord in the front on which can be hooked to the back of a motor boat, and then the fun begins.
3. On the order blanks you will see the different monograms in which are available.
4. Whitney told Rainsford of the mysterious island of which was the scene of many strange happenings.

5. Changing the ways of the world is normal, but changing some of the social roles of which men and women act out could upset the balance of society.

6. The child will assume the role for which it has been taught to act out.

7. We have a large clock on the wall in which our teacher watches very closely.

8. This is the building of which I know everything about.

8-2 Using which *and* that *to combine sentences correctly*

Directions: Combine each pair of sentences below by putting *which* or *that* between them and omitting any unnecessary words. Cross out the word you do not need. Then rewrite the sentence in the space provided.

Example: This is the stopwatch. You left ~~it~~ on the desk. This is the stopwatch that you left on the desk.

1. Her ability to listen is a valuable trait. It makes my mother a sympathetic person.

2. The story did not have the perfect ending. I had expected it to have such an ending.

3. The spider really is a harmless creature. I used to dislike it.

4. My aunt is always looking for antiques. She can put them in her living room.

5. Washing cars is a job. Bob does not particularly want it. ______________________

____

____

8-3 Avoiding the use of **who** *or* **which** *unless referring to a particular person or thing*

Directions: In the following sentences cross out *who* or *which* whenever it is incorrectly used to join complete thoughts. Then put a comma plus *and* above the correct word. (Do not change any sentences that use *who* or *which* correctly.)

Example: There are six rows of keys ~~which~~ , and each is labeled by number.

1. On the left side of the room is the door which one enters the classroom from it.

2. The person who was most like the hero was also a fighter.

3. We give dances which we charge a fee for admission.

4. I understand that he decided to call a meeting which that decision was certainly a mistake.

5. Many people feel that there is some misunderstanding involved which that the administration is trying to remove all students from the area in question.

6. She always looked to see if you were looking at her which if you weren't, she would leave the room.

7. It is an important decision which everyone has to make it at some time or other.

8. I have attached a two-sheet evaluation which I would appreciate your completion and return of this document by Tuesday, April 19, 1986.

8-4 Avoiding mixing up a statement and a question

Directions: Correct these sentences by following three steps: (1) insert *whether* or *if* as needed; (2) write an indirect question by putting the subject before the verb; and (3) change the tense of the second verb, if necessary.

Example: My sister wanted to know were we hurt anywhere. My sister wanted to know whether we were hurt anywhere.

1. My wife asked me was something the matter. ____________________

____

2. He wanted to know did I think I could find a job. ____________________

____

3. I asked Jessie did she feel that cool air. ____________________

____

4. Ronald wondered was there anything I needed. ____________________

____

5. I asked my neighbors had they seen anyone coming out of my house. ____________________

____

____

6. A couple of friends asked us was there a party. ____________________

____

7. I asked the bus driver did he put me off at the right stop. ____________________

____

____

8. I find myself wondering is this the place I grew up. ____________________

____

Directions: Rewrite each of the definitions given below. When necessary, add the class of the word to the first part of your definition.

Example: Halloween is when children in costumes go from door to door begging or playing pranks. *Halloween is a holiday celebrated by children in costumes who go from door to door begging for treats or playing pranks.*

1. The home plate in baseball is where each player has to touch in order to score a run. ____

2. Gossip is where one person is spreading rumors about another person. ____

3. Mimeographing is when you make several copies of a document by using a stencil, ink, and a roller. ____

4. The "pits" is when a person or situation is as bad or low down as possible. ____

5. The best animal trap is when a person digs a hole in the ground, fills it with sticks, and covers it over with leaves. ____

Directions: Rewrite the following sentences, giving each sentence a clear subject.

Example: By showing the public that criminals are punished can help to prove that it is not worthwhile to commit a crime. *Showing the public that criminals are punished can help to prove that it is not worthwhile to commit a crime.* or *By showing the public that criminals are punished, we can help to prove that it is not worthwhile to commit a crime.*

1. With today's modern weapons make war really horrifying. ____________________

2. By the addition of a student lounge and recreational facilities would help a great deal to ease the tension around the campus. ____________________

3. In taking the tables and chairs out of the room is only making things worse. ____________________

4. Just by looking at the scene reminded me of a place I would like to visit again some day. ____________________

5. By watching television keeps children from doing their homework. ______________

____

____

6. When we used that product increased our yield by 30 percent. ______________

____

7. Without thinking of the consequences caused many problems for the members of my family. ______________

____

____

8. In one of the brochures I once read stated that one of the prettiest waterfalls in the eastern United States is located in the Blue Ridge mountains. ______________

____

____

8-7 Avoiding mixed ideas

Directions: Decide what the writer wanted to emphasize in each sentence. Then rewrite the sentence.

Example: The tape is made from regular paper except for the size is much smaller than you would expect. The tape is made from regular paper except for its size. or The tape is made from regular paper, except that its size is much smaller than you would expect.

____

1. An example of dishonesty is trying to get out of a mistake that you know you made it yourself and letting someone else get blamed for it. ______________________

____

____

____

2. People forget that without companionship they won't be able to make it only if they turn to some substitute such as study or work. ______________________

____

____

____

3. An analysis of Browning's "The Bishop Orders His Tomb at Saint Praxed's Church" is a great descriptive poem. ______________________

____

____

____

4. In order to have companionship is to be easy to get along with. ______________________

____

____

5. After step four, go to number five is the hardest step of all. ______________________

____

____

6. Driving the back roads does not prove to be a safe driver. ______________________

____

____

8b
Cure your seriously mixed-up sentences.

8-8 Avoiding mixed-up sentences

Directions: Cure the following sentences. Decide what the writer means to say. Then rewrite the sentence, changing it so that its meaning is clear.

Example: Why I came to college is when I had three children, just about grown, but I was a young mother at twenty-one. Because I was a mother when I was twenty-one, I had to wait until my children were grown to go to college. or Because I had children when I was only twenty-one, I waited until they were grown to go to college.

1. Although the desk is used for sitting but the seats are still uncomfortable when you sit on them.

2. This particular day I was planning to go to school when the bus money was still on the bed.

3. One thing I have learned from this experience is that I should have my own key and to look inside my wallet before I leave.

4. The way to wash a sweater is first clean the sink if you are using it or a bathtub.

8c
Be sure that your sentences make sense.

8-9 Thinking about what you are saying

Directions: Change the following sentences so that they make sense.

Example: Turn the temperature on low by putting a teaspoon of butter in the skillet until it melts. *After turning the temperature on low, place the skillet on the burner, and wait for the butter to melt.* or *To melt a teaspoon of butter, put it in a skillet on the burner, and turn the burner temperature on low.*

1. Happiness is a state or quality which is a joy.

2. Looking at the blackboard in Room 217, I can see that the color is black.

3. There are many television programs on TV. ______________________________

____

4. Airplanes get you somewhere in half the time a car does. ____________________

____

5. Belonging to a military family, I got to see the world and hospitalization was free.

____

____

6. Florida is a nice place to visit for vacation because it has beautiful beaches, provided there are long summers. ______________________________________

____

____

7. School is the best start for a great future, for there are a few other sources for a good job without school. ______________________________________

____

____

8. The season of spring seems to give a beautiful feeling to all: boys, girls, men, and women. ____

____

____

CHAPTER NINE

Sentences with Misplaced and Dangling Parts

9a
Relocate the misplaced parts in your sentences.

9-1 Recognizing misplaced parts

Directions: In each group of sentences write the letter of the sentence that has no misplaced parts.

Example: A. Much studying is required in class along with homework.
B. Much studying along with homework is required in class. ___B___

1. A. I didn't know what I even wanted to study.
B. I didn't even know what I wanted to study. ______

2. A. The sailboat sliced through the waves with Bert at the tiller under full sail.
B. The sailboat, under full sail, sliced through the waves with Bert at the tiller. ______

3. A. I promised when he arrived I would work on the plans for the party.
B. When he arrived, I promised that I would work on the plans for the party. ______

4. A. Running down the stairs, I almost tripped on the ball.
B. I almost tripped on the ball running down the stairs. ______

5. A. Previously in excellent health, we were surprised to hear he was in the hospital.
   B. We were surprised to hear that he was in the hospital, previously in excellent health.
   C. We were surprised to hear that he, previously in excellent health, was in the hospital. ____________

6. A. We saw three kites high in the sky.
   B. High in the sky, we saw three kites.
   C. While high in the sky, we saw three kites. ____________

7. A. It was nearly the worst movie I ever saw.
   B. It was the worst movie I nearly ever saw.
   C. Nearly it was the worst movie I ever saw. ____________

8. A. He wore a dark green belt that matched his shirt which was patent leather.
   B. He wore a dark green, patent leather belt that matched his shirt. ____________

9. A. The business degree, which includes English, math, and economics, helps prepare students for many jobs.
   B. The business degree helps prepare students for many jobs which includes courses in English, math, and economics. ____________

10. A. Parkville, Ohio, is a small suburb of Cleveland with a population of less than 1,000 which is my hometown.
    B. Parkville, Ohio, is a small suburb, which is my hometown, of Cleveland with a population of less than 1,000.
    C. Parkville, Ohio, which is my hometown, is a small suburb of Cleveland with a population of less than 1,000. ____________

9-2 Correcting sentences with misplaced parts

Directions: Most of the sentences below contain misplaced parts. Rewrite the sentences, correcting the misplaced parts. If the sentence is correct, write *C.*

Example: She bought a rose from a saleswoman that was red. She bought a rose that was red from a saleswoman.

1. She answered the ad which appeared in Sunday's paper for a clerk. ____________

____

2. She bought a dress from a little shop made of denim. ______________________

____

3. John ran to the room where the teacher was giving the test with his heart pounding.

____

____

4. The cupcakes were given to the children that had vanilla icing on them. ____________

____

5. I said when the class was over I would tell her about it. ____________________

____

6. The hikers had to walk all day without sitting down to rest in the slushy snow.

____

____

7. The money has been returned that the robbers stole. ______________________

____

8. The dog which belongs to my neighbor buried a bone in my yard. ______________

____

9. I promised when the program was over that I would bake a cake. ______________

____

10. She wore a long, silk skirt with a peach blouse that was ankle-length. __________

____

9b
Give any dangling part in your sentences something to describe.

9-3 Recognizing dangling parts of sentences

Directions: Most of the following sentences contain dangling parts. If any underlined part of a sentence is dangling, write the number. If there are no dangling parts in a sentence, write *C* for correct.

Example: Swimming to the raft, (1) the water got stronger. (2) ___1___

1. Standing on the corner, (1) the woman's hat blew off. (2) ______
2. Fluttering in the breeze, (1) the laundry dried quickly. (2) ______
3. When only a small girl, (1) my mother took me to Europe. (2) ______
4. The sun set (1) while walking back to camp. (2) ______
5. The trip down river was exciting (1) to those riding the raft. (2) ______
6. The bell rang (1) while walking to class. (2) ______
7. The rain started (1) while we were at the bus stop. (2) ______
8. Crashing through the brambles, (1) the boy's shirt was torn. (2) ______
9. Lying in the hammock, (1) the grass was left uncut. (2) ______
10. Sleeping in the sun, (1) the dream awakened the dog. (2) ______
11. Driving in the country, (1) an old farmhouse was seen. (2) ______

12. Swimming in the gulf, my toe was cut on a rock. ________
1 2

13. With the success Chuck has had as a mechanic, I hope he will
1
become an air station supervisor soon. ________
2

14. When not understanding, a puzzled expression appears on his face. ________
1 2

15. After returning home, my family welcomed me with presents. ________
1 2

9-4 Recognizing dangling parts of sentences

Directions: In each of the following sentence groups only one sentence has no dangling parts. Write its letter.

Example: A. Wading into the creek, the water grew colder.
B. Wading into the creek, we found that the water grew colder.
C. The water grew colder wading into the creek. B

1. A. By typing neatly, your report will get a better grade.
   B. By typing neatly, you will get a better grade on your report.
   C. By typing neatly, a better grade will be given to your report. ________

2. A. While watching the parade, the elephants went by.
   B. While we were watching the parade, the elephants went by.
   C. The elephants went by while watching the parade. ________

3. A. Sleeping soundly, I was awakened by the phone.
   B. Sleeping soundly, the phone awakened me.
   C. The phone awakened me sleeping soundly. ________

4. A. After being under construction for two years, we finally moved into our new home.
   B. We finally moved into our new home after being under construction for two years.
   C. We finally moved into our new home after it had been under construction for two years. ________

5. A. While I was combing my hair, she arrived.
   B. Combing my hair, she arrived.
   C. While combing my hair, she arrived. ________

6. A. Aiming at the bull's-eye, the dart hit the wall instead.
   B. Although aiming at the bull's-eye, the dart hit the wall instead.
   C. Aiming at the bull's-eye, I hit the wall with my dart instead. ____________

7. A. Studying hard, the test was passed.
   B. The test was passed because he studied hard.
   C. The test was passed by studying hard. ____________

8. A. After tearing apart the garbage bags, I chained the dog.
   B. After it had torn apart the garbage bags, I chained the dog.
   C. I chained the dog after tearing apart the garbage bags. ____________

9. A. Running through the sand, I cut my foot on a shell.
   B. Running through the sand, a shell cut my foot.
   C. While running through the sand, a shell cut my foot. ____________

10. A. Since graduating from college, the company offered Tom a job.
    B. The company offered Tom a job since graduating from college.
    C. Since he graduated from college, the company offered Tom a job. ____________

9-5 Correcting dangling parts of sentences

Directions: Most of the following sentences contain dangling parts. If a sentence is incorrect, correct it. Begin your sentence with the underlined phrase. If a sentence is already correct, write *C.*

Example: Looking at the city lights, the scenery was beautiful. *Looking at the city lights, I found the scenery beautiful.*

1. Upon receiving the reward, the money was deposited in Joe's account in the bank.

____

____

2. Barking loudly, I was afraid the dog might not be bluffing. ____________

____

3. After cooking all day, the children surprised their mother with dinner out. ____________

____

____

4. Debating about grading policies, the issue was finally resolved. ______

______

5. Arriving early, many seats were available. ______

______

6. Flying through the clouds, the plane signaled to the tower. ______

______

7. Working all morning, the job was finally done. ______

______

8. While driving to school, the right front tire went flat. ______

______

9. As a lover of French food, that restaurant is my favorite. ______

______

10. By reading the poem carefully, the meaning becomes clear. ______

______

9-6 *Correcting dangling parts of sentences*

Directions: Most of the following sentences contain dangling parts. In the blank provided, correct the sentences by rewriting them. Use the underlined phrases in your new sentences. If a sentence is already correct, write *C.*

Example: Proofreading carefully, every error in the paper was corrected. ______

Proofreading carefully, he corrected every error in the paper.

1. Upon receiving the letter, tears filled her eyes. ______

______

2. Loafing in a hammock, the boy never finished his work. ______________________

____

3. Jim's pocket was picked, while standing in a crowd. ______________________

____

4. By discussing differences calmly, a solution was reached. ______________________

____

5. By using zip codes, you can help improve mail service. ______________________

____

6. While standing at the bus stop, it started to rain. ______________________

____

7. Gulping quickly, the coffee burned Mark's mouth. ______________________

____

8. The view was breathtaking, climbing to the top of the mountains. ______________________

____

9. That is still my favorite movie, even after seeing it yesterday for the tenth time.

____

____

10. Hanging on the living-room wall, you can see three landscapes. ______________________

____

11. Cooked to a crisp, the children did not like the cookies. ______________________

____

12. Eating quickly, the heavy meal gave me indigestion. ______________________

____

CHAPTER TEN

Nonparallel and Rambling Sentences

10a
Make the parts of your sentences parallel.

10-1 Identifying parts of sentences lacking parallel structure

Directions: If all parts of any of the following sentences are parallel, write *P* in the blank to the right. If they are not, underline the unbalanced part and then write its letter in the blank.

Example: John has problems (A) with reading, (B) remembering it, and (C) with writing. B

1. To get to Washington, a person may travel (A) by bus, (B) by airplane, or (C) ride in his own car. ________
2. On our trips my father often showed us (A) historic public buildings, (B) where the scenery was beautiful, and (C) modern museums. ________
3. (A) The placing of utility lines underground, (B) not allowing trucks, and (C) the expanding of bicycle routes would make an already good neighborhood even better. ________

4. When the children noticed that they were lost, (A) they stopped laughing, (B) their vitality declined, and (C) their speed slowed. ____________

5. Joe showed me (A) how to plow the ground, (B) how to plant the seeds, and (C) how to fertilize my garden. ____________

6. Sex-role stereotyping has frequently made women appear (A) passive, (B) dependent, (C) not strong, and (D) stupid. ____________

7. Although my neighborhood contains (A) spacious tree-lined boulevards, (B) beautifully landscaped yards, and (C) various recreational facilities, a few improvements are desirable. ____________

8. Few young men have had the opportunity to study such vocations as (A) how to cook, (B) nursing, or (C) hairdressing. ____________

9. The volcanic eruption required the people (A) to evacuate the small island, (B) that they return to the mainland, (C) and to seek aid. ____________

10. (A) Medicine, (B) law, (C) engineering, and (D) being interested in science have been considered men's fields for many years. ____________

11. By (A) keeping the lawn mowed, (B) trim the bushes, (C) and watering the grass occasionally, Mr. Allen keeps his yard looking very nice. ____________

10-2 Correcting parallel structure

Directions: None of the following sentences is completely parallel in structure. Rewrite each sentence, making sure to put the parts in parallel structure. Underline any words you change.

Example: Modern hospitals have a vast array of departments which are responsible for detecting, preventing, and to treat various illnesses. Modern hospitals have a vast array of departments which are responsible for detecting, preventing, and treating various illnesses.

1. Living in Portsmouth has many advantages, such as education, employment opportunities, social life, and centrally located.

2. If you want a snack and play some cards, just go to the lounge and have a good time.

3. Today's women are employed in the same jobs as men, no longer dress in a traditional way, and no longer act as they used to.

4. Police shows give people ideas about how to rob, drugs, and even murder.

5. The "unknown citizen" never caused anyone problems because he went to work every day, paying his dues, and he was socially accepted.

6. From watching television I know how a criminal can steal a car, rob a bank, kidnap a person, hide out in a vacant house, and how the criminal knows what tactics to use in

evading the police at the scene of the crime.

7. Calculators are used around the house to figure monthly bills, balance the checkbook, and useful when computing the income tax.

8. German shepherds are used to guard stores, junkyards, and you mainly see them at self-owned companies.

10-3 Using parallel structure

Directions: Copy the first sentence in each of the following pairs of sentences. Then complete the second sentence, using the new beginning given and following the pattern of the italicized words in the first sentence.

Examples: While fighting the fire I learned two things: *that I should not advance into a heavily burned building and that it is a painful experience to have a mask fail and fill with smoke.* While fighting the fire I learned two things: that I should not advance into a heavily burned building and that it is a painful experience to have a mask fail and fill with smoke.

While doing my homework I learned two things: that I must take better notes in class and that I must budget my time in order to complete all of my assignments.

1. To clean a handgun, all that is needed is *a cleaning rod, cleaning oil, and a silicone rag.*

____

____

To wash a car, all that is needed is ____

____

2. In a two-year college the conscientious student can *concentrate on an area of interest, take numerous electives, and continue to live at home.* ____

____

____

In extracurricular activities the interested student can ____

____

3. My plants are separated from nature by *the pots they live in, the window they grow by, and the room they are housed in.* ____

____

____

My house is separated from other houses on my street by ____

____

____

4. From television commercials Americans learn *the type of food to eat, the make of car to buy, and the brand of medicine to use.* ____

____

____

From magazine advertising Americans learn ____________________

____

____

5. After observing the stormy sea, I *returned to the protection of my tent, crawled into my sleeping bag, and thought about the power of the surf.* ____________________

____

____

____

After leaving the theater, I ____________________

____

____

10b
Give your sentences direction.

10-4 Writing sentences that do not ramble

Directions: Each of the following sentences contains unnecessary information that makes the meaning of the sentence unclear. Decide what the writer is trying to tell you. Then underline the unnecessary information. Rewrite the sentence, either leaving out the unnecessary information or putting it in a second sentence.

Example: Perhaps if we all stopped watching TV crime shows which would allow their ratings to drop, then maybe we could get a selection of television entertainment which does not teach crime or how to escape from the scene after a crime has been committed. Perhaps if we all stopped watching TV crime shows, we could get a selection of television entertainment which does not teach criminal activities.

1. A good example of forgetfulness occurs when a person who has a test one day and has studied the night before and gets to school and then tries to think exactly what the test is on and cannot do so. ______________________________

2. My favorite weekend recreation is bowling, especially with my family including my son who is two years old and very mischievous and usually distracts all of us by trying to roll the ball down the gutter which makes us all laugh. ______________________________

3. Children become angry with their parents a lot because they can't do what they want and have everything all the time and this causes everyone in the family to become upset with one another. ______________________________

4. I am in school to take some basic courses so I can improve my skills and go on to nursing school and continue what I hoped and planned so long only to have my hopes stopped several years back. ______________________________

CHAPTER ELEVEN

Guiding Readers

11a
Guide your readers so that they will know when events are happening.

11-1 Making clear when events are happening

Directions: In the following sentences change any italicized verb when necessary to make clear the time of the action. Then write the correct word in the blank to the right. Write *C* for any verb that needs no change.

Example: I *open*^ed my eyes and *saw* her sitting there. opened
C

1. When I get to my father's house I *notice* that it *had* changed. ______ ______
2. When Billy, Clyde, and Ken got in the building where I was hiding, they *called* but I *don't* answer. ______ ______
3. From a distance the apple seems perfectly shaped, but as I *approached* it, I *see* that it is very uneven. ______ ______
4. His objective is to sit and watch television, but after he

finished his supper, he *felt* he should help his father mow the lawn. ______

5. When Michael first met Lorraine, he *has* a warm feeling. ______
6. The movie is about four boys who *were* friends and *do* everything together. ______
7. My friend Sam goes to the beach where he *met* many interesting people who enjoy swimming, surfing, or just sunning. ______
8. In "The Most Dangerous Game," when Rainsford falls off the yacht, he *swam* and *found* his way to shore. ______
9. The largest component is the handle, and it *is* available in various sizes. ______
10. One day as Harry was traveling, he *sees* three people in a broken-down car who *need* help. ______

11-2 Making clear when events are happening

Directions: In each of the following sentences cross out the incorrect verb in parentheses. Then write the correct verb in the blank to the right.

Example: I was so enchanted by this woman that I (~~neglect~~, neglected) to ask an important but simple question. neglected

1. Jack the car up so that the wheel will come off after all the bolts (have, had) been removed. ______
2. After I had finished, I (begin, began) to put the grass in plastic bags. ______

3. There are large amounts of lead iron ore called taconite, but it (cannot, could not) be mined. ______

4. The fine powder was made into balls the size of marbles which (are, were) hardened to be used in blast furnaces. ______

5. After a few seconds the dogs (turn, turned) and left. ______

6. About two months ago I bought a car that looked good and (is, was) very clean. ______

7. After Mother died, Sam (leaves, left) home and joined the ______ Navy; when he returned, he (is, was) disappointed to find ______ everything (had changed, has changed). ______

8. I told him we were lost, and he (takes, took) us back to a main road. ______

9. Fishing is my favorite vice. I (love, loved) to fish. ______

10. Cecil was too old to keep up the chase, and the rabbit got away, so we (continue, continued) on our little hike. ______

11b
Guide your readers so that they will understand point of view. Be sure that they know who is telling about events, and to whom the writer is speaking. Avoid shifting person.

11-3 Using the same person

Directions: In the following sentences change any italicized pronoun when necessary to avoid shifting person. Then write the correct pronoun in the blank to the right. Write *C* if no change is needed.

Example: I always thought it would be exciting to earn ~~*your*~~ own paycheck. my

1. My children and I spend a lot of time in my bedroom because it makes *you* feel as if *you* are in a world all *your* own.

2. I am trying to work all day and go to college at night. This is sometimes hard when *you* get home from work at 4:30 and have to be at school by 5:00.

3. Keeping your eyes on the road is important in driving, but traffic is frequently so heavy that *a person* must watch the other cars constantly.

4. Math is hard for me to learn because *I* have no background in it, but when *you* have teachers that are patient, *you* feel better in class.

5. After a few hours a person becomes sleepy and tired of driving, but when traveling at speeds of 50 and 60 m.p.h., *you* have to keep alert.

6. Dr. Brown is my family physician. She checks *your* temperature and measures *your* pulse.

7. My favorite way to spend a weekend is traveling from place to place. I really like traveling when *you* have a friend along who loves the highway as much as *you* do.

8. Jack could still remember *his* mother's old gray stove. *You* had to wait at least fifteen minutes for the oven to heat, and it was so old *he* couldn't find any replacement parts for it.

9. The climb to the top is an exciting one because the higher we climb, the more *your* ears begin to pop, and from the top *you* can see for miles and miles. ________________ ________________

10. Looking around, I see some older people like me who seem to be doing well in school. *I* know now that if *you* keep up with *your* homework, *anyone* can succeed in college. ________________ ________________ ________________ ________________

11-4 Using the same person

Directions: Complete the following sentences by using the correct pronouns.

Example: I know Mr. Smith loves his work; ____I____ can tell from the expression on his face.

1. Hicksville was our hometown, but the schools were so crowded ________________ often had over thirty children in each of ________________ classes.

2. When you have a flat tire on the highway, you must be able to jack up ________________ car, remove and replace the defective tire, and place it in ________________ trunk.

3. It's not that you've been out of school too long or that ________________ don't want to learn, but it takes a while to change a routine ________________ have had for years.

4. If you live close to your job, walk to work. Walking is not only good exercise, but it also enables ________________ to find out about the world around ________________. Also, just think of all the money ________________ can save if ________________ walk instead of drive to nearby places.

5. I can still remember going to the old fairgrounds when ________________ was a child. The minute ________________ entered the gate ________________ got a feeling of excitement.

6. When a student needs improvement in some of his writing skills, it really hurts ________________ to miss many days in a quarter.

7. I love to fish. It's beautiful when ________________ can sit out in an open lake.

8. When you live twenty miles from school and ________________ get home from work at five o'clock, ________________ don't have much time to get ready and get to ________________ evening class on time.

11c
Guide your readers so that they will know whether you intend your writing to be serious, funny, sad, or exciting.

11-5 Making clear the feeling you wish to express

Directions: Rewrite the following paragraph so that the reader will not be confused about the ideas and feelings it expresses.

The President has established a new workweek for American workers in the hope that the new working hours will stimulate productivity. The new workweek will begin on Monday morning at eight o'clock and end on Thursday evening at six o'clock—thank goodness for Thursday! This system will let American employees work Monday through Thursday, leaving Friday through Sunday for them to goof off. This seems like a great plan; besides, it can't hurt even if it doesn't help.

____

____

11d
Guide your readers so that pronoun references are clear.

11-6 Giving a clear reference for **it, they, them,** *or* **that**

Directions: Cross out the italicized pronoun that does *not* clearly refer to a person or thing. Then insert one or more nouns to make the meaning clear.

Example: In my family ~~*they*~~ my parents have a rule about our coming home before midnight.

1. As I was walking past the corner of Elm and Main, *that* reminded me of a scary movie.
2. According to the story, *they* are all looking for happiness and contentment.
3. Though they try hard to please everyone, *they* always find people who are unahppy with the food.
4. As the dog started to bark at the kitten, I grabbed *it.*
5. All you card sharks who spend your free time playing cards in the cafeteria should sign up for *them* in the tournament.
6. When I return a book to the library, *they* always look at its due date.

7. Drive up to the entrance, and the valet will park *it* for you.

8. Now that I have a job, I can buy things without having to ask *them* for the money.

9. I like to unpack crates because I can see *them* before all the other people do.

10. He did fairly well in his courses last quarter, but *they* were even higher this quarter.

11-7 Giving only one possible reference for a pronoun

Directions: If the italicized pronoun in each sentence below clearly refers to a person or thing named in the sentence, write *C* in the blank to the right. If the reference is unclear, rewrite the sentence so that the reference is unclear.

Example: If students consulted more with their teachers, *they* might get to know them better. ________

If students consulted more with their teachers, the teachers might get to know them better.

1. While living overseas, I learned many things. I was especially interested in learning what the Turkish people believe and how *they* live. ________

____

____

2. The ship's sail was small, but *it* went fast. ________

____

3. Sometimes students complain that teachers expect them to know material that *they* have not covered in the text. ________

____

____

4. My car has an automatic shift *that* makes you feel as though you're about to take off at a very high speed. ____________

____

____

5. Things have been different in school since Melvin and Joe left. *They* have really changed. ____________

____

____

6. During the snowfall of early February, the city was virtually at a standstill because *it* caught the city off guard. ____________

____

____

7. Adolescents shouldn't ignore their parents' advice because *they* are there to guide *them.* ____________

____

____

8. My favorite TV show is "Hill Street Blues" because *they* really act their parts. ____________

____

____

9. An employee will produce more work for a congenial foreman because *he* feels part of the organization. ____________

____

____

10. My apartment is not comfortable; in the living room *they* have a gas heater which is supposed to heat five rooms. ______________

____

____

11-8 Using singular and plural words clearly

Directions: In the following sentences cross out any pronoun whose reference is not clear. Then write the clear reference above the crossed-out word. (For related exercises see 6b.)

Example: Several citizens of Portsmouth recently received commendations for ~~its~~ *their* clean-up efforts.

1. In this city houses don't have to be inspected before it can be rented.
2. The child in a large family has a lot of people to tell him what to do, but they have many people to help them also.
3. Show dogs are trained to obey its master as commands are given.
4. In making ceramics, molds are used for giving it shape.
5. The employees don't feel motivated to do their best work because there is a barrier between him and the manager.

CHAPTER TWELVE
Spelling

12a
Learn the simple rules of spelling.

12-1 Changing final y *to* i *before adding some endings*

Directions: If *y* is immediately preceded by a consonant, change *y* to *i* and add the ending. If *y* is immediately preceded by a vowel, add the ending. Keep the *y* before adding *ing.* In the following sentences fill in each blank with the correctly spelled form of the words in parentheses.

Example: I was happier __________ than he was last night. (happy)

1. Yesterday I __________ two hours for the test. (study)
2. I have been __________ at this college for one year. (study)
3. Henry __________ each day and so do I. (study)
4. Winning the marathon was the __________ moment of Tina's life. (happy)
5. I __________ all weekend about the speech I had to give on Monday. (worry)
6. Who is your __________ at your summer job? (employ)

7. Are you going to be __________________ the whole summer? (employ)

8. My friend's company __________________ over 500 people now. (employ)

9. A person with no skills may not be __________________. (employ)

10. My class schedule still __________________. (vary)

11. He is __________________ her in June. (marry)

12. They have been __________________ for six years. (marry)

13. This is the __________________ job I've ever had. (easy)

14. It certainly is __________________ than the last one. (easy)

15. He was __________________ too many books and dropped one. (carry)

16. Right now he __________________ a course load of 18 hours. (carry)

17. Don't get __________________ away when you watch the game today. (carry)

18. He has been __________________ his job so far. (enjoy)

19. Lee __________________ his last job also. (enjoy)

20. In fact, he finds many types of jobs very __________________. (enjoy)

12-2 Using ie *or* ei

Directions: This rhyme often helps to remind spellers of the correct use of *ei* or *ie*:

> Use *i* before *e* except after *c*,
> and when sounded like *a* as in *neighbor* and *weigh*.

Put *ei* or *ie* in each blank to complete correctly the words in the following sentences. Exceptions to the rule include height, weird, neither, and seize.

Example: She stocked up on food as if we were about to be under s___ie___ge.

1. We saw three deer standing in the f_________ld.

2. I was rel_________ved when the test was over.

3. Did you rec_________ve an invitation to her graduation?

4. My nephew and n__________ce are visiting us for a few days.

5. He has been a close fr__________nd of mine for seven years.

6. What is the h__________ght of that new building downtown?

7. That movie was too w__________rd for me to enjoy.

8. It is my bel__________f that people aren't born prejudiced.

9. It is normal to go through a period of gr__________f after the loss of a loved one.

10. N__________ther Henry nor Mark could come.

11. You must bring your rec__________pt with you in order to return a book.

12. My next-door n__________ghbor has three dogs.

13. You must s__________ze the opportunity for success when it comes.

14. He felt a drip and looked up at the c__________ling to find the leak.

15. Did you punish your child for trying to dec__________ve you?

16. The ch__________f reason I took the course is that the subject interests me.

17. Did she perc__________ve the change in the furniture arrangement?

18. The police caught the th__________f the day after the robbery.

19. He is the most conc__________ted person I know.

20. I could not conc__________ve of doing such a thing.

12-3 Using the endings **-ent** *and* **-ence,** *and* **-ant** *and* **ance**

Directions: In each of the following sentences cross out the incorrect word or words in parentheses. Then write the correct word or words in the blanks to the right.

Example: What is the (~~different~~, difference) between a Raleigh bicycle and a Fontan bicycle? *difference*

1. Ice skating and roller skating are (different, difference) in many ways. __________

2. It is very (important, importance) to follow directions carefully. ____________

3. Having the trip go smoothly was of great (important, importance) to me. ____________

4. This is a very (important, importance) occasion. ____________

5. It was (evident, evidence) that more (evident, evidence) ____________ was needed to solve the case. ____________

6. A hair dryer is a modern (convenient, convenience) that most people now consider a necessity. ____________

7. The nearness to the library was a (convenient, convenience) aspect of the class. ____________

8. A nurse must have a lot of (patient, patience) to work ____________ with some difficult (patients, patience) in the ward. ____________

9. The fact that he could learn the new job so quickly showed that he was (intelligent, intelligence). ____________

10. The fact that he did well on the difficult test revealed his (intelligent, intelligence). ____________

11. An (intelligent, intelligence) person often has a great deal ____________ of (confident, confidence). ____________

12. He is such a (confident, confidence) person that he in- ____________ spires others to have (confident, confidence) in him. ____________

13. I am (confident, confidence) that your (confident, confidence) in John will be rewarded. ____________

12-4 *Dropping the final* e *before a vowel ending*

Directions: Usually when a word ends in silent *e*, drop that *e* before adding an ending that begins with a vowel. However, keep the *e* before adding an ending that begins with a consonant. In each of the following sentences cross out the incorrect word in parentheses. Then write the correct work in the blank to the right.

Example: (Using, U~~seing~~) a flashlight to see, Sue caught a glimpse of the strange creature. *Using*

1. Try to be especially (careful, carful) as you drive on holiday weekends. ________
2. Fay is always (hopful, hopeful) of finding a steady job. ________
3. (Hateing, Hating) to do homework made Jim dislike school. ________
4. My (adoreable, adorable) canary likes to perch on my finger. ________
5. This (comeing, coming) summer my younger brother will be nine years old. ________
6. During Lisa's first year away from home, she was dreadfully (homsick, homesick). ________
7. David keeps (believing, believeing) that he can pass the course. ________
8. Butch seems to enjoy playing those (hateful, hatful) jokes. ________
9. My neighbor owns and trains several (homeing, homing) pigeons. ________

10. Paul's father always leaves his work promptly at (closing, closeing) time. ____________

12-5 Choosing a single consonant or double consonant before an ending

Directions: Usually when a word has a short vowel sound as in *hop*, you double the consonant before endings beginning with a vowel (*hopped*). When the word has a long sound as in *hope*, you do not (*hoped*). In each of the sentences below choose the correctly spelled word or words in parentheses. Then write the correct word or words in the blanks to the right.

Example: They were (tapping, taping) the TV show. taping

1. He was (hoping, hopping) to get to see a rabbit (hoping, hopping) along. ____________ ____________
2. Stop (hoping, hopping) up and down, and tell me what is wrong. ____________
3. He was (hoping, hopping) to get a raise. ____________
4. My sister's hair was all (mated, matted). ____________
5. I (mated, matted) my Doberman with a Pekingese. ____________
6. He was (sloping, slopping) water from the bucket all over the floor. ____________
7. The steeply (sloping, slopping) roof kept the snow from collecting. ____________
8. I couldn't keep from (taping, tapping) my foot in time to the music that the band was playing. ____________
9. Norman was busily (taping, tapping) name tags in all his books. ____________

10. He (striped, stripped) off all the old paint before starting to refinish the chest. ________

11. Her (striped, stripped) blouse matched her skirt. ________

12. Jeff (pined, pinned) for her the whole time they were apart. ________

13. Alice had (pined, pinned) all the pattern pieces on the material and was ready to begin cutting. ________

14. It is difficult to find a person who still does an old craft such as chair (caning, canning). ________

15. My friend does a lot of (caning, canning) when his tomatoes are ripe. ________

12b
Use a hyphen (-) to join words and numbers.

12-6 Using a hyphen

Directions: In each sentence decide which words, if any, need hyphens. Then write the hyphenated word or words in the space provided. Write *C* if no hyphens are needed.

Example: The old man was said to be over ninety five. ninety-five

1. She had on a lavender hat, a printed scarf, and a pale blue suit. ________

____

____

2. The self service pumps are cheaper than the full service ones. ________

____

3. The well known writer turned out to be an ordinary looking, middle aged woman.

4. We found that one third of the students in the class agreed with the proposed slate of officers.

5. The blue green glass in the windows and the wrought iron balcony gave the restaurant an exotic appearance.

6. The thin lipped, sixty eight year old woman rocked the chubby faced, blue eyed baby on her knee.

7. The wire haired terrier ran alongside the bright eyed, happily laughing child.

8. The steadily chiming clock told us that the end of the evening was rapidly approaching.

9. The gradually setting sun cast a reddish orange glow over the valley.

10. Her tightly curled, blonde hair gave a doll like appearance to her girlishly round face.

12-7 ***Separating words into syllables***

Directions: Being able to separate words into syllables is a great help for clear pronunciation and correct spelling. In the exercises below separate the words into syllables wherever possible. Then write these syllables in the blanks to the right.

A. For this exercise remember: Each syllable has only one vowel sound.

Example: baseball ___base ball___

reading ___read ing___

depth ___depth___

1. classroom ________________
2. indeed ________________
3. corridor ________________
4. breakfast ________________
5. wear ________________

B. For this exercise remember: If a single vowel is followed by a consonant and another vowel, the separation usually comes after the first vowel. That vowel often has a long sound.

Example: final ___fi nal___

remember ___re mem ber___

1. minus ________________
2. private ________________
3. procedure ________________
4. open ________________
5. pilot ________________

C. For this exercise remember: If a single vowel is followed by two consonants and another vowel, the separation usually comes between the two consonants.

Example: running — run ning

number — num ber

1. offense ______

2. petty ______

3. common ______

4. igloo ______

5. master ______

D. For this exercise remember: If a word ends in *le* preceded by a consonant, the separation usually comes before that consonant. If a vowel ends the first syllable, that vowel is often long.

Example: purple — pur ple

trouble — trou ble

1. fable ______

2. maple ______

3. able ______

4. cattle ______

5. marble ______

E. For this exercise remember: Vowel and consonant blends usually stay together.

Example: pronounce — pro nounce

phonograph — pho no graph

1. jacket ______

2. caution ______

3. poison ____________________

4. enchant ____________________

5. secret ____________________

12-8 Review

Directions: In the exercise below separate the words into syllables. Remember the suggestions for the exercises you have just completed.

1. cricket ____________________
2. quitter ____________________
3. terrible ____________________
4. bookstore ____________________
5. myrtle ____________________
6. height ____________________
7. April ____________________
8. inkwell ____________________
9. rabbit ____________________
10. march ____________________
11. counter ____________________
12. secure ____________________
13. influence ____________________
14. motion ____________________
15. courage ____________________
16. migratory ____________________
17. extemporaneous ____________________

18. manufacture ______________________

19. inference ______________________

20. independent ______________________

CHAPTER THIRTEEN

Commas and No Commas

13a
Use a comma and a coordinating conjunction (*and, but, or, nor, for, so, yet*) to separate two main clauses.

13-1 Using commas and the coordinating conjunctions **and, but, or, nor, for, so, yet** *to separate main clauses*

Directions: The following sentences are made up of two main clauses separated by *and, but, or, nor,* or *for.* Insert a comma in any sentence that needs it. Then underline the word before the comma, the comma, and the word after the comma. If a comma is not needed, write *C* in the blank to the right.

Examples: His eyebrows are dark and heavy, but his hair is reddish-brown. __________

I like football, but I think basketball is more fun to play. ___C___

1. The children ran across the street without looking at the traffic but the cars managed to stop in time. __________
2. The walls in the room are a very light blue, and the shag carpet is just a little darker than the walls. __________
3. The twin boys have never dressed alike nor do they look alike. __________

4. The morning classes fill up very rapidly at registration time for that is when most of the students prefer to go to school. ____________

5. There are many types of stores in my community but there are only a few that I find convenient for my shopping. ____________

6. Most compact cars give very good gas mileage and are easy to park because they don't need much space. ____________

7. I have tried doing some writing but something always seems to interrupt me, and I never do finish any of my stories. ____________

8. If you are going to refinish a piece of furniture, you must first remove all of the old paint or varnish or you can just put on a fresh coat of paint for a hurry-up job. ____________

9. A driver must be very cautious when he is driving on ice or snow and he should use some of the same care when driving on a wet road. ____________

10. Sometimes I think I would like to be one of the characters I'm reading about, but, if the story has a sad ending, I'm better off just being myself. ____________

13b

When a dependent clause beginning with conjunctions like *after, although, because, if, when,* and *while* starts a sentence, place a comma between it and the main clause.

13-2 Using commas between dependent clauses and main clauses

Directions: The following sentences are made up of main clauses and dependent clauses. Insert a comma in any sentence that needs it. Then underline the word before the comma, the comma, and the word after the comma. If a comma is not needed, write *C* in the blank to the right.

Examples: If Randy doesn't play in the next game, we may not make it to the finals. ________

We may not win the game if Randy isn't able to play. C

1. While the container is open add all of the other ingredients at one time. ________
2. After class is over, take all of the papers to Margie. ________
3. Although the salary is rather small the job will furnish both experience and references. ________
4. History class always causes me a lot of trouble because I can't seem to remember dates and places. ________
5. When the conditions at home are considered it is very surprising that the two children perform as well as they do in school. ________
6. After I went to New York I never again felt content with life in a small town. ________
7. While the rain poured down the roof started to leak, and the wind blew two window shutters loose from their hinges. ________

8. If the houses in the area are ever going to look any better someone will have to apply some paint and clean up the yards. ____________

9. After the dog across the street has barked all night, I'm just too tired to get up early the next morning and go to class. ____________

10. The playgrounds in the city need both volunteer and paid helpers this summer if the proposed program is to be completed. ____________

13-3 Review of commas with main and dependent clauses

Directions: Copy the following paragraph, adding commas where needed.

When I arrived at the airport I became very nervous again and my friends had to keep me from going right back home. After they talked to me for a while I decided to go on with my trip but the seat belts nearly made me change my mind again. I wanted to be able to jump out before the plane crashed if the pilot had any trouble. I finally fastened the belt and closed my eyes while the plane started to move down the runway. When I opened them again I couldn't believe what I saw. The plane was moving smoothly along and I could see the land just as though it were a map below the plane.

____

____

____

____

____

____

____

____

13c
Use commas between the words or groups of words in a series or list.

13-4 Using commas in a series

Directions: Insert commas where needed in the following sentences. Show where a comma has been added by underlining the word before the comma, the comma, and the word after the comma. If no commas are needed, write *C* in the left margin.

Example: My uncle has two dogs, five cats, a parakeet, and a large goat.

1. Remember to take pencils paper and all of the books to class.
2. Now add two cups of flour three eggs a cup of milk and a teaspoon of vanilla flavoring.
3. Put the cat out turn off the television and close the door.
4. There were two cars in the driveway, and both of them had flat tires broken headlights and dented fenders.
5. An interest in nice clothing a newly acquired taste for expensive food and rapidly expanding inflation caused a sudden drop in my bank balance.
6. Guard dogs that bark ferociously jump threateningly and snarl viciously usually frighten away intruders.

7. Disciplined skillful even-tempered German shepherds make splendid Seeing Eye dogs.

8. In addition, these dogs make friendly, loving pets if they are trained to be with children.

9. German shepherds are found everywhere: in cities towns farming communities and mining areas.

10. Many thoughtful, considerate people believe that a dog is man's best friend.

13d

Use commas between adjectives such as *large, small, dark, beautiful, exciting,* and *noisy* in place of the word *and*. If *and* cannot be used, a comma is not needed.

13-5 Using commas with adjectives

Directions: Copy the following sentences, inserting commas where needed. If sentence is correct, write *C* in the blank.

Examples: She wore a shabby wrinkled coat and muddy shoes. She wore a shabby, wrinkled coat and muddy shoes.

When the brilliant red car swerved around the corner, I had to jump for my life. C

1. I didn't think I would be happy living in that creaky old house. ____________________

2. A small frisky cat leaped out into my path. ____________________

3. Every one of the tired old women jumped up and ran toward the windows. ____________

____

____

4. The painting was small and delicate, but the frame was dark and heavy. ____________

____

____

5. He had on a dark blue sweater and torn baggy pants. ____________

____

____

13e, f

Use commas to set off, or separate, the name of a person to whom you are speaking and to separate the names of speakers from their exact, or quoted, words.

13-6 Using commas with the name of a person speaking or spoken to

Directions: Insert commas where needed in the following sentences. Show where a comma has been added by underlining the word before the comma, the comma, and the word after the comma. If the sentence is correct, write *C* in the blank.

Examples: With slow, slurred words, Mr. Dawson said, "You'd better try to locate my son and his wife." ____C____

Take that dog out of the house, Jenny, and don't let it back in here. ____________

1. My intention Mrs. Thompson is to give you an adequate explanation of the whole matter. ____________

2. "Do you think" yelled my sister "that you'll get away with something like that?" ______

3. Marion take this book to your mother and ask Carolyn about the tickets for the play. ______

4. "I just can't believe it John" said Uncle Charlie. "I never thought you would decide on such a plan." ______

5. We had thought, Tammy, that you would stay with us for another month. ______

6. Jump up on the chair George and give me the large dish on the top shelf. ______

7. "When you came in" said Francis "I didn't recognize you for several minutes." ______

13g
Use commas to separate the parts of names, places, dates, and addresses.

13-7 Using commas with place names, dates, and addresses

Directions: Copy the following sentences, inserting commas where needed to separate place names, dates, and addressed. If any sentence is correct, write *C* in the blank.

Examples: The summer session begins on Thursday June 8. The summer session begins on Thursday, June 8.

Brownsville, Texas, was his home for many years. C

1. We lived in Denver Colorado for two years, and then we moved back to Oregon.

______

2. The house at 4310 Colley Avenue had been torn down, and my old hometown didn't seem the same any longer.

3. The road to Summersville West Virginia now crosses New River, giving the traveler a spectacular view.

4. Many of the people living in Columbus Ohio were not even aware of the events planned for the first Monday in August.

5. My sister lives at 6213 Plainsfield Street Henson Michigan, and I plan to rent a house on Remson Avenue which is just two blocks away.

6. The first Friday in June was an important day in my life.

7. May 28 1986 will probably mark the end of my college days.

8. Send the package to 1803 Eastwood Street St. George Utah 25701 by the last of this week.

9. We are going to Oceanside, California, for our vacation next month.

10. My friends head for the ski slopes at Stowe Vermont nearly every weekend during the winter. ______________________

____

13h

Use commas to separate a word or group of words that give nonessential information about a person or thing.

13-8 Using commas with a word or words that are not essential (can be omitted) to the meaning of the sentence

Directions: Insert commas where needed in each of the following sentences. Then copy the comma or commas and the words separated. If the sentence is correct, write *C*.

Examples: My school, which is the largest in the area, offers many different courses during the day and evening. , which is the largest in the area,

Mr. Jones, my neighbor, always has a smile and a greeting for everyone.

C

1. Everyone cheered as Bill the boy in the orange jacket ran toward the finish line.

____

____

2. Lucille the tall girl on the right is one of my best friends. ______________________

____

3. The papers that were turned in were graded and returned the next day. ______________________

____

____

4. A job that offers many fringe benefits may be better than one with higher pay.

____

____

5. We remembered to take the blue suitcase, but we forgot the red one which was still standing in the hall. ____

____

____

13-9 Using commas around a **who** *or* **which** *expression (relative clause) when it is not essential to the meaning of the sentence*

Directions: Insert commas where needed in each of the following sentences. Then write the words separated by the commas and the commas in the space provided. If the sentence is already punctuated correctly, write *C.*

Examples: That road, which I travel every day, passes right by the college. C

My summer vacation, which I have been waiting for, begins with a visit with you. , which I have been waiting for,

1. Summer days which pass quickly find my friends and me at the beach sunning or surfing. ____

2. Surfing which I like best is most exciting when the wind is blowing exactly right and the waves are high. ____

3. Lying on the sand and feeling the sun's rays which sometimes get too hot is my idea of relaxing. ____

4. Many of our friends from school who also enjoy the summer join us for a fast game of volleyball on the beach. ____

____

5. When the activity is over, we all enjoy a picnic lunch which we prepared earlier before we leave our favorite summer playground. ______________________________

____

6. Next summer, which seems far away now, we will probably do the same things.

____

13-10 Using commas with transitional words or expressions such as **therefore, for example, as a result, meanwhile, on the other hand,** *and others*

Directions: Insert commas where they are needed in each of the following sentences. Then underline the word before the comma and the word after it. If the sentence is correct, write *C* in the blank.

Examples: My plan, in fact, is to get all my work finished before I leave today. ___C___

I will try to finish all my work as soon as possible; meanwhile, have patience with me. ________

1. By the way are you coming to my graduation exercises? ________
2. I would like to attend the ceremonies, but on the other hand I would also like to play softball with my team. ________
3. It seems as a matter of fact that I frequently have to choose between two things to do. ________
4. Last week for example I had to choose between attending John and Liz's wedding and Pete and Sylvia's wedding. ________
5. However in order not to offend either couple, I attended neither of the weddings. ________
6. My friends understood my dilemma; nevertheless I felt cheated. ________

7. As a result I have been very careful to make people aware of my need to attend the affair of my choice. ________

8. It must be apparent, therefore, that I have not yet decided which event I will attend. ________

13-11 Using commas to separate introductory clauses or prepositional phrases which contain participles or infinitives from the rest of the sentence

Directions: Insert commas where needed in each sentence. Then underline the words separated by commas. If the sentence is correct, write *C* in the blank.

Examples: After deciding on the topic, the next step you must take is to write down any ideas you have about it. ___C___

Thinking that he was right, the student argued his point effectively. ________

1. Believing that he was late for class John drove rapidly down the highway. ________

2. Even driving as carefully as he did he narrowly missed being involved in a collision. ________

3. Looking up suddenly my friend noticed a speeding compact car coming toward him. ________

4. After making a hasty survey of the situation, John pulled over to the right side of the road. ________

5. Unknown to John the person in the car immediately behind him did the same thing, however. ________

6. Glancing quickly out the side window John noticed that the car which had been behind him was almost parallel to his car. ________

7. Greatly agitated the young man reacted quickly and veered off to the left just after the speeding car passed. ____________

8. Counting his blessings John was able to steer the car back to the right and resume at a normal speed. ____________

9. In order to pull himself together he stopped his car at the next gas station. ____________

10. Unable to think of anything but his narrow escape John did not attend his class after all. ____________

13i–13q
Use commas to make your meaning clear; do not use unnecessary commas.

13-12 Review

Directions: The following paragraph has too many commas. As you carefully read it, decide which commas are not needed. Then rewrite the paragraph in the space provided.

Several movies, that are now playing at local theaters are based on science fiction. Two of them, seem to be especially popular. *E. T.*, the story of a young boy's adventure with, a being from another planet, has been playing for almost two months. People continue to come, to see the film. In addition, the theater showing *Return of the Jedi* has large crowds continuously. Some people think that this story about wars in outer space, is frightening. However, unusual creatures, horrifying warfare, mysterious places, and large, incredible machines, seem to catch people's imagination. These things make them forget, themselves for a while, although they must eventually return to reality.

CHAPTER FOURTEEN

The Semicolon

14a
Use a semicolon between two main clauses that are closely related.

14b
Use a semicolon before a connecting word that introduces a main clause.

14-1 Using a semicolon to join sentences

Directions: If a semicolon is not needed in a sentence below, write *C* in the blank to the right. If a semicolon is needed, either add it or change a comma to a semicolon. Then underline the word before the semicolon, the semicolon, and the word after the semicolon.

Example: I planted the tulips in the front yard; there is no more room in the back. ________

1. We waited twenty minutes for him, however, he never came. ________
2. We had planned to stay outdoors, however, the rain forced us in. ________
3. I called his name twice. However, he did not hear me. ________
4. Math is not an easy subject for me, therefore, I must spend a lot of time on it. ________

5. She worked hard, therefore, she passed the course with a B. ____________

6. It is, therefore, necessary to start over at the beginning. ____________

7. I don't really enjoy softball, nevertheless, I play in order to go along with the group. ____________

8. He had a good recommendation and previous experience, as a result, he got the job. ____________

9. She tried to sew in a hurry and, as a result, the dress did not fit properly. ____________

10. Working while attending college is not easy, it can be done only if a person is motivated. ____________

11. First assemble all the ingredients you will need, then put the sugar and eggs into a bowl. ____________

12. Many types of hobbies are challenging, for instance, sailing demands concentration and skill. ____________

13. I planned to be ready at 7 A.M., instead, I didn't wake up until 8 and had to skip breakfast in order to catch the bus. ____________

14. Jerry mowed the lawn, meanwhile, I did the trimming. ____________

15. She moved to California six months ago, still, we consider ourselves close friends. ____________

14c
Use semicolons between groups of words that already contain commas.

14d
Do not carelessly use a semicolon instead of a comma.

14e
Do not confuse the semicolon and the colon.

14f
Do not use a semicolon unless you have a reason for it.

14-2 Using semicolons correctly

Directions: In each group of sentences one sentence is punctuated correctly. Write its letter in the blank to the right.

Example: A. I was tired after staying out late, but I got up early the next day anyway.
B. I was tired after staying out late; but I got up early the next day anyway. ____a____

1. A. While I clipped the hedges; he finished mowing the lawn.
   B. While I clipped the hedges, he finished mowing the lawn. ________

2. A. Although it was nearly 9:30, we still went out to dinner.
   B. Although it was nearly 9:30; we still went out to dinner. ________

3. A. You will need the following items; clear Contac paper, some pictures from magazines, and a pair of scissors.
   B. You will need the following items: clear Contac paper; some pictures from magazines, and a pair of scissors. ________

4. A. The officers elected were Martha Jones, president, Bob Swift, vice president, Mae Watford, treasurer, and Dan Fisher, secretary.
   B. The officers elected were Martha Jones, president; Bob Swift, vice president; Mae Watford, treasurer; and Dan Fisher, secretary.
   C. The officers elected were; Martha Jones, president, Bob Swift, vice president; Mae Watford, treasurer; and Dan Fisher, secretary. ________

5. A. I tried to phone him three times, however, he was never home.
   B. I tried to phone him three times; however, he was never home.
   C. I tried to phone him three times however; he was never home. ____________

6. A. After studying for four hours, I had to take a break.
   B. After studying for four hours: I had to take a break.
   C. After studying for four hours; I had to take a break. ____________

7. A. The parts assigned in the play were Tom, the doctor, Margaret, the mother, Joe, the father, and Kathy, the young girl.
   B. The parts assigned in the play were Tom; the doctor; Margaret; the mother; Joe; the father, and Kathy; the young girl.
   C. The parts assigned in the play were Tom, the doctor; Margaret, the mother; Joe, the father; and Kathy, the young girl. ____________

8. A. We put the roast in the oven, set the timer, and got out the ingredients for the vegetable dishes, then we were ready to start dessert.
   B. We put the roast in the oven; set the timer; and got out the ingredients for the vegetable dishes; then we were ready to start dessert.
   C. We put the roast in the oven, set the timer, and got out the ingredients for the vegetable dishes; then we were ready to start dessert. ____________

9. A. While he set the table, I got everything ready to serve even though the guests hadn't arrived yet.
   B. While he set the table; I got everything ready to serve even though the guests hadn't arrived yet.
   C. While he set the table, I got everything ready to serve; even though the guests hadn't arrived yet. ____________

10. A. Many years ago my neighborhood consisted of three homes; my parents', my sister's, and mine.
    B. Many years ago my neighborhood consisted of three homes: my parents', my sister's, and mine.
    C. Many years ago my neighborhood consisted of three homes, my parents'; my sister's and mine. ____________

11. A. Now the car is ready to be washed; because everything is wet.
    B. Now the car is ready to be washed, because everyting is wet.
    C. Now the car is ready to be washed because everything is wet. ____________

12. A. I headed for the storm cellar and waited until the storm was over.

B. I headed for the storm cellar, and waited until the storm was over.

C. I headed for the storm cellar; and waited until the storm was over. ____________

CHAPTER FIFTEEN

The Apostrophe

15a
The apostrophe shows that something belongs to or is related to something else.

15-1 Using the apostrophe to show possession

Directions: In the following sentences add apostrophes to any words that need them. Then write the correct words in the blanks to the right.

Example: Bobs face is fat and square. Bob's

1. Now that I am back in school, I have trouble doing all the things I am used to doing in a days time. ________
2. At 0900 hours, the ships company was called to attention. ________
3. A pipe fitters job is very interesting. ________
4. Her eyelashes are always curled up, not straight like everybody elses. ________
5. I made a small table with chairs for my sisters daughter. ________
6. The college is within a short distance of ones home. ________
7. Homer agreed to do a days work. ________

8. My neighbors house was remodeled recently. ________________

9. I can still remember the day I got my drivers license. ________________

10. Be sure to have the babys clean diaper ready. ________________

15-2 Using the apostrophe to show possession

Directions: In the following sentences cross out the incorrect words in parentheses. Then write the correct words in the blanks to the right.

Example: My (sisters, sister's, sisters') personality is charming. sister's

1. Sometimes Kay drives her (brother's, brothers) car, and sometimes she drives her (sisters, sister's). ________________

2. I like to share other (people's, peoples') problems. ________________

3. Knowing Mr. (Jones', Jone's, Jones) temper, I never argue with him. ________________

4. We talked with the doctors about several (patients, patient's, patients') behavioral patterns. ________________

5. Let's compare the two (states, state's, states') characteristics. ________________

6. He has sparkling eyes that attract (peoples, people's, peoples') attention. ________________

7. In my (neighbor's, neighbors') yards were many beautiful flowers. ________________

8. Television has had a devastating effect on some of (todays, today's, todays') children. ________________

9. The amount of tuition charged sometimes is based on a families', familys, family's) income. ________________

10. The sports car came speeding right into my (mothers, mother's) truck. ____________

15b
When pronouns end in *one* or *body*, they are treated like nouns. To make them show possession, add *s*.

***15-3 Using the apostrophe with such words as* anybody, everybody, nobody, *and* everyone**

Directions: In the following sentences add apostrophes to any words that need them. Then write the correct words in the blanks to the right. If no apostrophes are needed, write *C.*

Example: I can't wear just anybody's clothes. anybody's

1. We watched everyones plate to see who really was the biggest eater. ____________
2. Rainsford met the hunter who was nobodys friend. ____________
3. Yvonne will listen to anybodys troubles. ____________
4. Someones book was left in the classroom. ____________
5. Everyone feels like quitting sometimes. ____________
6. She has a face that catches everybodys eye. ____________
7. Nobody seems to understand my problems. ____________
8. When she came into the room, Jane noticed someones coat on her chair. ____________
9. Jack listened to everybodys story before he made a decision. ____________

10. As it turned out, the accident was nobodys fault. ____________________

15c
If something belongs to two or more people use *'s* with only the last of the two names.

15-4 Using 's after the last name when something belongs jointly to two people and after each name when things belong to each one separately

Directions: Correct the following sentences. Write *C* in the blank if no *'s* is needed.

Example: Harry and Susan daughter is older than Lynn or Tom sons. Harry and Susan's daughter is older than Lynn's or Tom's sons.

1. After his son and daughter-in-law deaths, Gus Ritter didn't live long. ____________

2. Carolyn and Bill new house is over on the other side of town. ____________

3. Who would have believed that Phil and Lisa dog would win the prize! ____________

4. Sandra and Beth best friend is Pam. ____________

5. That huge dog belongs to John and Bridgette. ____________

6. Bob dog and Cathy cat get along very well. ____________

7. John and Michael cars are both in good condition. ______________________________

____

8. My mother-in-law and sister-in-law recipes are always good. ____________________

____

9. Both the plant and the tree leaves fell during the storm. _______________________

____

10. Success of the new product is assured because of Frank Smith and his wife endorsement. ____

____

15d
The apostrophe is used to show omission

15-5 Using the apostrophe to show omission

Directions: In each sentence cross out the incorrect words in parentheses. Then write the correct work in the blank to the right.

Example: I (~~dont~~, don't, ~~do'nt~~) put on a front to try to impress people. don't

1. I (cant, ca'nt, can't) fool her about my days off. ______________
2. I (could'nt, couldn't, couldnt) move out, even though all my friends had left me. ______________
3. (Thats, That's, Thats') the only time he is ever sensible. ______________
4. The plant also has two buds that (have'nt, haven't, havent) bloomed. ______________

5. (Lets, Lets', Let's) hop on the next train. ____________

6. (Dont, Don't, Do'nt) forget your bait because without it ____________
   you (wont, wo nt, won't) catch any fish. ____________

7. The bus left the school at nine (oclock, o'clock, o clock)
   that Friday. ____________

8. Most of the time (Im, I'm) so tired I (dont, don't, do'nt) ____________
   feel like coming to class. ____________

9. That really (isnt, isn't, is'nt) the way to finish the job. ____________

10. I'm almost certain that Jesse, our beloved dog, (would've,
    wouldv'e, wouldve) come if I had called more loudly. ____________

15-6 Avoiding incorrect use of apostrophes

Directions: In each sentence cross out the incorrect forms in parentheses; then write the correct form in the blank.

Example: Then I have to come back to reality, knowing (~~its'~~, it's, ~~its~~) just a dream. *it's*

1. Women of yesterday wore their better dresses only on (Sundays, Sunday's, Sundays'). ____________

2. When I have a good day, (its, it's, its') unusual and unexpected. ____________

3. I couldn't believe how run-down the (house's, houses, houses') were. ____________

4. Because of (it, its, it's) low tuition the college is especially popular with low-income students. ____________

5. Even though I pretend that this car is mine, I know it's really (there's, their's, theirs). ____________

6. Kelley has gleaming brown (eye's, eyes', eyes). ____________

7. I can still recall that old stove with (its, it, its') dull gray color. ____________

8. My aunt (refuse's, refuses, refuses') to love the (one's, ____________ ones' ones) who really need her. ____________

9. (Its, It's, Its') my home now, and it (looks, look's, looks') ____________ like a palace to me. ____________

10. All of the (employee's, employees', employees) will go out of their way to help. ____________

15-7 Review

Directions: Copy the following paragraph, adding apostrophes where needed.

My brothers face always has a smile on it. Its a welcome sight to see. Hes the kind of person who loves to meet people and make new friends. He was one of the most popular graduates in the Class of 74, and he still doesnt have any enemies. My brothers warm personality helps his business. Jims Rent-All. In fact, his customers are really friends who dont mind helping out if theyre needed. My brothers such a likeable person that even his in-laws cant dislike him!

____

____

____

____

15-8 Review

Directions: As you carefully read the following paragraph, notice that many of the words can be contracted. Decide which can be and then write the contractions in the space provided. (Note that this paragraph is informal. Contractions are usually unacceptable in formal writing.) Some lines have no or more than one possible contraction.

Fixing a flat tire is not all that difficult if you have the ______
proper tools and if you proceed carefully. (It will probably ______
be necessary to get your hands dirty, of course.) Do not ______
attempt to do anything, however, until you are certain that ______
you have set the brake. Remember that there is always a ______
possibility that the car might move if you do not do this. ______
The tools that you will need are the jack, the handle, and ______
the wrench. After you have set up the jack, then you will ______
need to pump the handle several times to raise the car so ______
that it does not touch the pavement. This should be done so ______
that you are able to turn the wheel easily. Using the wrench, ______
turn each of the nuts clockwise. They will probably be dif- ______
ficult to loosen; however, when they are loose, you will be ______

able to unscrew them all the way, and they will slip off the bolt. Now remove the tire. It would be nice to think that all you would have to do is slip on the spare tire from the trunk. However, that will only be possible if you have remembered to keep the spare tire in good condition. If you have done so, slip the spare onto the wheel, tighten the nuts, and take the car off the jack. Then you are ready to drive away.

CHAPTER SIXTEEN

Quotation Marks

16a

When the exact words of a writer or speaker are repeated, these words are called a direct quotation and must be indicated by enclosing the person's words in quotation marks.

16-1 Using quotation marks for a person's exact words

Directions: In the following sentences, insert quotation marks, capital letters, and commas where needed. If no change is necessary in a sentence, write *C* in the blank to the right.

Examples: She said that she would be late. ___C___

She said, "I will be late." ________

1. She asked whether our cat had new kittens. ________

2. She asked if our cat had new kittens. ________

3. She asked does your cat have new kittens? ________

4. Did he say he was ready? ________

5. Did he say that he was ready? ________

6. Marie whispered to her cousin the tall boy is your blind date. ________

7. Mother shouted, Tom, come to the window and look at me! ________

8. Mother, shouted Tom, come to the window and look at me! __________

9. Jerry yelled, look out for the window, as the batter hit the ball. __________

10. John wondered if the job would ever be done. __________

16b

Use quotation marks to enclose the titles of short stories, songs, articles in magazines, parts of books, and short poems when they are referred to in other written material. (The titles of complete books or magazines and other long works are underlined or italicized.) Do not enclose the title of your own paper in quotation marks.

16-2 Using quotation marks for minor titles

Directions: In the following sentences, insert quotation marks where needed. If no change is necessary in a sentence, write *C* in the blank to the right.

Example: Did you read "Peanuts" last Sunday? __________

1. Did you know that Simon and Garfunkel's song Richard Cory is based on a poem by Edwin Arlington Robinson? __________

2. Their other songs such as Bridge over Troubled Water and The Dangling Conversation are also like poems set to music. __________

3. Is The Night the Ghost Got In your favorite Thurber short story? __________

4. Did you know that there was a movie based on Poe's story The Black Cat? __________

5. Is the article How to Train Your Dog as good an example of a process paper as How to Grow African Violets? __________

6. Is the Hallelujah Chorus your favorite part of Handel's *Messiah*? __________

7. My friend Marcy has read Faulkner's story The Bear more than ten times. ____________

8. After seeing *South Pacific*, I thought I would never stop humming Bali H'ai and Some Enchanted Evening. ____________

9. Is If Ever I Would Leave You, from the musical *Camelot*, one of her favorite songs? ____________

10. Conrad's story Youth really was based on his own experiences. ____________

16c, d
In addition to a person's exact words and minor titles, you may use quotation marks for uncommon nicknames, well-known expressions, and words used as words.

16-3 Using quotation marks for nicknames, well-known expressions, and words used as words

Directions: In the following sentences, insert capitals, quotation marks, and any other marks of punctuation where needed.

Example: The words "wander" and "wonder" have entirely different meanings and pronunciations.

1. The words pin and pen sound similar.
2. Did you and the Whiz Kid get all A's again?
3. When I thought it over, I realized for the first time what more haste, less speed meant.
4. The word stature should not be confused with statue or statute.
5. Did you know who said give me liberty or give me death?
6. Were you ever called teacher's pet in elementary school?

7. His yacht was really just a rowboat.

8. I was happy to see that in my paper I no longer confused lose with loose.

9. In some parts of the country, the word feel is pronounced almost the same as fill.

10. Do the people in your hometown pronounce aunt the same as ant?

11. Almost everyone knows what the word extraterrestrial means after seeing the popular movie *E.T.*

CHAPTER SEVENTEEN

The Period and Other Marks

17a

Use a period to end a statement, a request or an indirect question, and after most abbreviations.

17-1 Using a period to end a statement

Directions: In the following paragraph insert a capital letter at the beginning of each sentence and insert a period at the end of each sentence.

Example: college is different from high school in many ways in college you have the right to go full time or part time this is something you decide on in high school you are given a certain time to attend classes there are many other differences, too

vans are becoming increasingly popular among young people there are many reasons for this the first reason is that vans are useful young people feel in many cases that the vans are like small house trailers with the prices of automobiles constantly rising, young people believe that they get more for their money when they buy a van a second reason for the popularity of vans is that young people like to be involved in making new styles popular, like CB radios and casual clothing probably these are the most important reasons for the rising popularity of vans

17-2 *Using a period to end a sentence that requests something, makes a statement, or is an indirect question*

Directions: Insert a capital letter at the beginning of each sentence, and insert a period at the end of each sentence. Then tell whether the sentence is a *statement*, a *request*, or an *indirect question.*

Example: ~~m~~My friend asked me if I would take her to the store. indirect question

1. being independent means being self-sufficient in every way ____________
2. please return the library books before they are due ____________
3. pass the papers to the front of the room ____________
4. most household tasks are easier to do today than they were fifty years ago ____________
5. my brother wondered if I would help him do his mathematics problems ____________
6. most retired military men and women are very proud of their contributions to the United States ____________
7. his next-door neighbor asked John if he would help move some furniture ____________
8. read your themes carefully before handing them in ____________
9. my mother always wants to know where I have been whenever I'm late getting home from my classes ____________
10. skiing is a sport that requires patience and perseverance ____________

17-3 Using a period after most abbreviations

Directions: Put periods where needed in the following sentences. Underline any periods you insert. If a sentence is correct, write *C* in the left margin next to the sentence.

Example: Mr. and Mrs. Earl P. Jones have recently moved to West Virginia.

1. Shortly after 9 A M the students began to walk into the room.
2. Dr. L B Jones opened a dental office in downtown Richmond last month.
3. According to my history book, the city of Rome fell in 476 A D after numerous attacks by its enemies.
4. Because the invitation included R S V P, I wrote a note saying that I would attend Bette's party.
5. Watching TV is my favorite pastime.
6. Lt Peter J Lynch, Jr, is expected to report for active duty with the U S Navy at 1 P M on Monday, June 11, 1984.

17b
Use a question mark to end a question.

17-4 Writing questions

Directions: Change the following statements into questions. Then supply the correct end punctuation.

Example: Many people believe that elk are an endangered species. Do many people believe that elk are an endangered species?

1. All the assignments have been completed. ______________________________

____

2. Anger can be caused by a misunderstanding between two people. ______________

____

3. One way to define tolerance is to give several examples of it. ______________

____

4. My job at the meat-packing plant is interesting because it varies almost every day.

____

____

17-5 Using question marks correctly

Directions: At the end of each sentence insert a question mark or a period; then underline the punctuation mark. Write *direct question* or *indirect question* in the space to the right, depending on which punctuation mark you have used.

Example: The professor inquired whether I was making progress in writing my term paper. *indirect question*

1. Why did the class end so early ______________
2. John asked Marge if she would attend the lecture with him ______________
3. The librarian wondered if I had an identification card with me ______________
4. What's the biology assignment for our next class ______________
5. The registrar asked when I would complete my application ______________
6. Are you planning to attend summer school ______________
7. Have you completed the requirements for your degree ______________
8. Sometimes the instructors ask what your reactions to the assignments are ______________

9. Do you ever ask yourself whether or not you are going to reach your goals ______________

10. Even the most ambitious students ask when their assignments will be less difficult ______________

17c
Use an exclamation point at the end of a sentence that shows strong feeling or surprise or one that gives a strong command.

17-6 Using the exclamation point

Directions: In the following sentences supply the correct end punctuation. Then indicate which punctuation mark you used.

Example: Help! I can't swim! exclamation point

1. Call the police immediately ______________
2. Please come and sit down ______________
3. Leave this room immediately ______________
4. When can you have your assignment completed ______________
5. Whoa Stop that runaway horse ______________
6. Hold that line ______________
7. Come quickly The class has already begun ______________
8. Go away I have work to do ______________
9. Complete your assignment ______________
10. Oh The water is overflowing ______________

17d
Use the colon correctly.

17-7 Using the colon

Directions: Put in colons where needed in the sentences below. Underline the added colons. Write either *call attention* or *separate* to show why you inserted each colon.

Example: Here are the winners of the field events**:** Marvin Morse, Alvin Frisch, Buddy Thomas, and Hughie Smith. call attention

1. The campus opens at 700 A.M. ______________
2. My goals in life are three success, contentment, and wealth. ______________
3. Jarret has one serious problem the lack of money. ______________
4. Genesis 11 begins the story of creation. ______________
5. These are my most difficult courses chemistry, English, and trigonometry. ______________
6. Last spring John identified three kinds of birds mockingbirds, robins, and cardinals. ______________
7. The meeting scheduled for 130 P.M. actually began at 200. ______________
8. Sally has three sisters and a brother Joan, Betsy, Lisa, and Ken. ______________
9. George has one favorite pastime arguing. ______________
10. While flying to California in a DC10, I noticed three geographical features the dense forests, the rolling plains, and the rugged mountains. ______________

17e, f, g
Use dashes, parentheses, and brackets correctly.

17-8 Using dashes, parentheses, and brackets

Directions: Insert dashes, parentheses, and brackets where needed in the following sentences. Write *D* if you used dashes, *P* if you used parentheses, and *B* if you used brackets.

Example: His three brothers--Peter, Don, and Mark--are all skating champions. D

1. All of my friends except Mary are in my history class. ________
2. Parentheses are used to enclose 1 certain words, 2 figures, or 3 letters. ________
3. Mark Twain Samuel Clemens wrote *The Adventures of Huckleberry Finn.* ________
4. My son merely a child to me has returned home qualified to be a U. S. Army pilot. ________
5. The distressed woman anxiously called, "Bobby, who must be her son come here this minute." ________
6. Lecturing to his geology class about natural resources, the professor said, "Unless something is done about it conserving natural resources I guess we will soon deplete our supplies." ________
7. Spinach supposed to be good for us is not one of my favorite foods. ________
8. The new class actually a workshop has attracted many students. ________

17-9 ***Review of periods, question marks, exclamation points, dashes, parentheses, and brackets***

Directions: Insert punctuation marks in the following paragraph. Underline any punctuation marks that you add.

Refinishing a piece of furniture cracked with age like mine seems to be easy if you assemble these materials 1 furniture stripper, 2 clean cloths, 3 sandpaper, 4 a spray can of lacquer Do not ask yourself whether or not you can do the job Be confident that you can succeed if you follow these directions First apply one or two coats of paint stripper. Then wipe off the old, loosened paint. Next, sand the surface vigorously Mr P F Lewis, Jr, my guide in these matters, has often said, "Although sanding furniture is difficult and sometimes boring an understatement if I've ever heard one it's absolutely essential for refinishing antiques successfully" When you've completed the sanding, you're ready to apply the lacquer Spray a thin coat and let it dry Then spray another Finally your piece is finished Aren't these instructions easy to follow Surprise

CHAPTER EIGHTEEN

Capitals

18a
Capitalize the first word of a sentence.

18b
Capitalize proper names.

18-1 Using capitals at the beginning of a sentence and with proper names

Directions: Add capital letters where needed in the following sentences. Write the newly capitalized words in the blanks to the right. Some blanks may not be used.

Example: Our family dentist is dr. Raymond a. billings. Dr. / A. / Billings

1. My curriculum calls for one more course in english and two more in history. ______ ______

2. Last august we visited western North Carolina and camped in the Great Smoky mountains for two glorious weeks. ______ ______

3. Bill daniels hopes to become a doctor, but he still has three years of study at a medical college ahead of him. ______ ______

4. the children in the audience laughed and applauded as bugs bunny raced across the screen at the neighborhood theater.

5. The catholic church on broad street has a large day-care center for three-year-old children.

6. her attorney, Harmon collins, plays golf every saturday morning with my brother.

7. Warren and bernice have some beautiful pictures that they took in the jungles of brazil.

8. Three police cars came rushing to the scene of the accident after a green cadillac nearly ran over that little red volkswagen.

9. When i last saw uncle Fred, I was only seven years old.

10. Thanksgiving day is always on thursday, but christmas may be any day of the week.

11. Pictures and souvenirs from world war II are on display in the little museum over on Pleasant avenue.

12. All of the papers must be sent to the commonwealth national bank before the first of next month.

13. If you want an interesting course, why don't you try sociology 326? ____________

18c

Capitalize the first, last, and important words in the titles of books, movies, television programs, record albums, tapes, plays, songs, and poems. Capitalize the second part of important hyphenated words. Do not capitalize short prepositions, short conjunctions, or *a, an,* or *the*.

18-2 Capitalizing words in titles

Directions: Insert capital letters in the titles in these sentences. If any sentence is correct, write *C* in the blank to the right.

Example: Marlon Brando's best role may be Stanley Kowalski in *A Streetcar* N *named Desire.* ____________

1. It took me three weeks to read *war and peace*, and I still was not able to spell the names of any of the characters. ____________
2. The band completed the concert by playing "under the double eagle." ____________
3. I'll never forget playing the part of Emily in a college production of *our town.* ____________
4. Some of the students were very unhappy when the class was required to learn a long poem with the title of "when I finally go back to my old mountain shack." ____________
5. My favorite Beatles' hit is probably "Hey Jude." ____________
6. John Steinbeck wrote *of mice and men.* ____________

7. The latest ballad composed by our class poet is called "the cat in the ladder-back chair." ____________

8. Marge and Juanita have their tickets for *the mother-in-law*. ____________

9. Was Leonard Nimoy in the television series *Star Trek* or in the movie *Star Wars*? ____________

18d
Capitalize *I* when it is used as a word.

18e
Capitalize the first word of quoted sentences.

18-3 Capitalizing I *and the beginning of quoted sentences*

Directions: Insert capital letters where needed in the following sentences. If a sentence is correct, write *C* in the blank to the right.

Example: The announcer said, "W will everyone please move forward to the starting position." ____________

1. "when will you have your assignment ready?" the professor asked. ____________

2. Nearly everyone in the room stood up and yelled, "let's go, team!" ____________

3. Paul said that he would be here before noon. ____________

4. The third paragraph states, "after the old finish is removed, sand the wood until it is smooth. then begin to apply the stain, being careful to wipe off any excess liquid as you go." ____________

5. "Take the car around to the back door," said my father, "and put the boxes and bags on the back seat. then put the two suitcases in the trunk." ____________

6. The article on water pollution relates some very sad stories about human carelessness and lack of concern. ____________

7. "Fasten your coat and get something over your head and ears," Mr. Jones called. "now jump up and down to keep warm." ____________

8. "I am going," said the small boy, "because i think that one of us needs to be there." ____________

18-4 Review

Directions: Insert capitals where needed in the following paragraph. Call attention to each capital added by underlining the word.

Example: When I saw bill last tuesday, he looked very strange.

when evening comes, i am happy to head for home because i have a room of my own for study and recreation. I have worked since last november to make it just right, and now it is always ready for me. a carpenter helped me with some of the complex work, and bill and randy came in every thursday to give me a hand. Mason lumber company delivered everything promptly; however, they sent the wrong material two different times. But at last it is finished, and i can say with sincerity as i step through the door, "it's beautiful to be home."

18-5 Review

Directions: The writer of the following paragraph was not always sure when she needed capital letters. Proofread her paragraph, marking an X through any error and writing your corrections in the margin.

Aunt Agnes's house

Last Wednesday, i decided to find my Aunt Agnes's new house in Auburn as I had never visited her there. The only clues I had about location were that she lived on main street and that she was never known for her neatness. accompanied by my Friend Sarah, i paraded up and down main street, searching for Agnes's House. Glancing through a window, Sarah said, "look! This must be Agnes's house. Through the living room window I can see clothes all over the floor and a Baldwin Piano on which are piled many back copies of the *Courier Journal*, several *TV guides*, a pair of dirty socks, and a copy of *David Copperfield*. Through the kitchen window I see dirty dishes on the frigidaire and in the sink." I agreed immediately. "Yes," I replied. "the evidence is overwhelming. This is indeed where Agnes lives."

CHAPTER NINETEEN

Underlining, Abbreviations, and Numbers

19a

Underline the titles of books and some other published materials; titles of works of art; television series; films; record albums; names of ships, trains, and other special vehicles; and some words when you refer to them in your papers.

19-1 Underlining titles and names

Directions: In each sentence underline any title or name that needs underlining. Then write the underlined name or title in the blank to the right. If the sentence is already correct, write *C.*

Example: We read A Doll's House by Henrik Ibsen in English class. *A Doll's House*

1. The movie Airport frightened my cousin so much that she called off her vacation trip to Hawaii. ______
2. My sister reads *Science* from cover to cover each month. ______
3. The paintings by Degas were her favorites of all she saw at the art museum. ______

4. Van Gogh's The Starry Night is one of Joshua's favorite paintings. ____________

5. I just read a terrible book entitled Wolves at the Door. ____________

6. Gladys and Trina are going to take a cruise to the West Indies on the ship Carousel. ____________

7. Tickets for the play Sensational cost eighteen dollars. ____________

8. One of my cousins has seen Star Wars at least fifteen times. ____________

9. We all went to the Palace Theater to see the new play. ____________

10. Ritchie thought Madame Butterfly was about insects. ____________

19-2 Underlining words, letters, and figures

Directions: In each sentence underline any word, letter, or figure that needs underlining. Then write the underlined word, letter, or figure in the blank to the right. Write *C* if the sentence is already correct.

Example: Circle every 7 on the page. ______7______

1. Do not use the word pass when you mean that something has already happened. ____________

2. My definition of the word happiness may be quite different from yours. ____________

3. I don't like to use the green typewriter because the n looks just like an *r*. ____________

4. Many people find joy in very simple things. ____________

5. The word manager was misspelled three times on the first page. ____________

19b

Abbreviations are shortened versions of names or titles and are often used where there is not much space.

19-3 Using abbreviations

Directions: In each sentence cross out the incorrect choice in parentheses. Then write the correct choice in the space to the right.

Example: I saw (Mr., ~~mister~~) Jones at the store. Mr.

1. All of the (Sts., streets) in the area near the park have been torn up for weeks. __________
2. The program lists (Capt., Captain) Richardson as the main speaker for the evening. __________
3. Please be there no later than 7 (P.M., post meridian). __________
4. Springhill (Ave., Avenue) is the prettiest, cleanest street in town. __________
5. Our (Dr., doctor) never makes a house call anymore. __________
6. The travelers had to use horses (&, and) wagons for the long trip across the prairies. __________
7. More people live in (Calif., California) than in any other state. __________
8. The English class meets only on (Tues., Tuesday) evening at the library. __________
9. All of the onions are in five (lb., pound) bags. __________
10. I almost failed my last (hist., history) course, but Sandra made a good grade and didn't study at all. __________

19c
Spell out most numbers that can be expressed in one or two words. Use a hyphen with compound numbers.

19-4 Using numbers and numerals

Directions: If any of the following sentences uses numbers or numerals correctly, write *C* in the blank to the right. If the usage is not correct, underline the error and write the correction.

Example: Our neighbors have seventeen cats and 3 dogs. three

1. My father has 5 brothers and 8 sisters. ________
2. Do you watch the soap operas on Channel 2? ________
3. 23 books have disappeared from the library this semester. ________
4. Her uncle lent her $six hundred for her books and tuition. ________
5. Due to inflation, the price of a very ordinary house is now around fifty-five thousand, five hundred dollars. ________
6. I never can remember whether a mile is 5,280 feet or 2,850 feet. ________
7. He was born on June twenty first, 1942. ________
8. Some banks are now paying 10 percent interest on money in special savings accounts. ________
9. Send the package to five twenty-nine Sunset Lane. ________
10. 9:15 is the starting time for your class. ________

19-5 Review

Directions: Add quotation marks or underlining as needed.

My three sisters are all quite different in their musical and literary tastes. Lois, the oldest, spends hours at the piano working on her ragtime favorites by Scott Joplin such as The Entertainer, The Easy Winners, and The Maple Leaf Rag. She also enjoys pieces from musicals such as Dulcinea and The Impossible Dream from Man of La Mancha. In addition, she is a Neil Diamond fan, playing Sweet Caroline, America, and You Don't Bring Me Flowers while we all sing along. Her reading taste runs to science fiction classics such as the novels Dune and The Time Machine as well as Demian by Herman Hesse.

Janet, the middle sister, doesn't play an instrument but sounds just like Barbra Streisand when she sings Evergreen. Her favorite reading consists of poems such as Tennyson's In Memoriam, Matthew Arnold's Dover Beach, and Browning's My Star. She also enjoys longer classical works such as Vivaldi's The Four Seasons, Horst's The Planets, and Bach's Brandenburg Concerto No. 3. Her favorite opera is Puccini's La Boheme.

Frances, the youngest, enjoys satirical works such as Tom Lehrer's So Long, Mom, We're Off to Drop the Bomb, Pollution, and National Brotherhood Week. Fantasy works including Tolkein's The Hobbit and Mary Stewart's trilogy on Merlin the magician–The Crystal Cave, The Hollow Hills, and The Last Enchantment–are her favorite types of fiction. Frances has a great sense of humor, so Thurber's short stories such as The Night the Ghost Got In and The Catbird Seat are favorites of hers as well as Mark Twain's stories The Lightning Rod Man, The Diary of Adam and Eve, plus The Story of the Bad Little Boy. She also enjoys his longer works such as Roughing It, Life on the Mississippi, and, of course, the classic The Adventures of Huckleberry Finn.

Even though their tastes differ, all three sisters agree that music and literature add a great deal of pleasure to their lives.

CHAPTER TWENTY

Learning to Use the Dictionary

20a
Learn to find the words you want to use.

20-1 Using a dictionary to find word meanings

Directions: Write the letter of the best answer in the space to the right. Be sure to consult a dictionary first.

Example: *Deftness* is (A) a hearing loss (B) skill. B

1. What would you find living in an *apiary*? (A) apes (B) bees (C) soldiers (D) children ______
2. What is an *estuary* part of? (A) a body of water (B) a blood vesses (C) a land mass (D) a college ______
3. Where would you be most likely to find a *gazebo*? (A) in a zoo (B) in an airplane (C) in a garden (D) in an orchestra ______
4. Which is the correct relationship between a *dearth* of something and a *plethora*? (A) the first is a small amount and the second is a large amount (B) the first is a large amount and the second is a

small amount (C) both refer to small amounts (D) both refer to large amounts ____________

5. Where would you be most likely to find an *egress*? (A) in a theater (B) in a tree (C) in a dam (D) in a tropical climate ____________

6. Where would you be most likely to find *extraterrestrial* life? (A) in the sea (B) on another planet (C) in a cave (D) on a dog ____________

7. A *charlatan* is a (A) fake (B) color (C) lizard (D) gymnast ____________

8. *Nickel* is (A) a ten-cent piece (B) a metal (C) a pest (D) a girl's name ____________

9. If something is *flagrant*, it is (A) playful (B) obvious (C) waving (D) sweet-smelling ____________

10. If you refer to the *result* of something, is it the (A) effect (B) affect? ____________

11. If you devote a lot of *effort* to a job, you (A) expand (B) expend a lot of energy. ____________

12. Natives are said to be (A) indigenous (B) indigent to a country. ____________

20b
Learn the kinds of information given in a dictionary.

20-2 Using a dictionary for pronouncing and dividing words and for spelling

Directions: Use an standard dictionary to answer the following questions.

Example: Which of the words *quit* and *quite* has a long vowel sound? (Hint: The long vowel says its name.) quite

1. What are the two correct pronunciations for *respiratory*? ______________________

____

2. What other spellings are acceptable for these words?

A. judgment ______________________ D. canvased ______________________

B. traveling ______________________ E. alright ______________________

C. counselor ______________________

3. Is the word for an engaged woman pronounced differently from the word for an gaged man (fiancé), and, if so, how? ______________________

4. What syllable of the word *frequent* is accented when it is a verb, and what does the verb *frequent* mean? ______________________

5. Show where you would use a hyphen if you needed to divide the following words at the end of a line. If a word cannot be divided, write *no* in the blank.

A. committee ______________________ D. recipe ______________________

B. frequency ______________________ E. relevant ______________________

C. coast ______________________

6. Write *one* in the blank if any of the following terms are written as one word and *two* if it is two separate words. If the term is hyphenated, write it with the hyphen.

A. room mate ______________________ D. entrance way ______________________

B. motor home ______________________ E. sail boat ______________________

C. book keeper ______________________ F. self conscious ______________________

7. In the blanks to the right write the letter of the correct pronunciation for each of the following words.

Example: résumé (A) re ZOOM (B) RAY zum ay ____B____

benign (A) bee NINE (B) bee NIG ______________

facsimile (A) Fak SE me lee (B) fa SE me lee ____________

saccharin (A) SACH a rin (B) SACK a rin ____________

8. Write the number of the syllable that is accented in each of the following words.

Example: antithesis ___2___

superfluous____________ extemporaneous ____________

automaton ____________ macadam ____________

9. Write the letter or letters that are silent in each of the following words.

Example: gnat ___g___

psychologist ____________ fillet ____________

knee ____________ subtle ____________

parfait ____________ buffet ____________

space ____________ neighbor ____________

pneumatic ____________ know ____________

20-3 Using a dictionary for information about irregular verb forms

Directions: A dictionary lists verb forms with the present tense first (without the *s* ending), followed by the irregular simple past and then the participles used with helping verbs *have* and *be.*

Example: drive (drīv) *vt.* drove, driv′en, driv′ing

simple past (drove) — used with helping verb (driv′en, driv′ing)

If no verb forms are listed, the verb is regular (takes the *-ed* ending). Use any standard dictionary to find the answers to the following questions:

Example: What is the simple past form of drive? ___drove___

1. What are the simple past verb forms of the following verbs?

A. swim ____________ C. grow ____________

B. fly ____________ D. tear ____________

E. choose ____________________ G. set ____________________

F. see ____________________ H. lie ____________________

2. What is the correct verb form in each of the following sentences?

Example: We have swum there before. (swim)

A. I have ______________ the bracelet. (break)

B. He has ______________ up all the glue. (use)

C. The balloon has ______________. (burst)

D. He has ______________ movies of famous stars. (film)

E. We had ______________ all the coffee. (drink)

F. They had ______________ the foundation for the house. (lay)

G. Jack has ______________ speeches before. (give)

H. My sister has ______________ that dress only once. (wear)

I. Mrs. Mitchell had just ______________ down when the phone rang. (lie)

20-4 Using a dictionary to learn how and when to use a word

Directions: Using your dictionary, locate the label explaining when and how to use–or *not* to use–each of the following words. Then copy from the dictionary the word, its label, and its meaning.

Example: right (when used to mean *very*)

right : archaic, extremely.

1. gismo ____________________

2. whilst ____________________

3. go-ahead ____________________

4. gyp ____________________

5. Jim Crow ____________________

6. jive ______________________________

7. jitterbug ______________________________

8. jitters ______________________________

9. cool ______________________________

10. thou ______________________________

11. gee whiz ______________________________

12. footman ______________________________

13. hype ______________________________

14. prizer ______________________________

15. frontless ______________________________

20c
Use a dictionary to spell words correctly.

20-5 Using a dictionary to correct misspelled words

Directions: In the blank to the right write the letter of the correctly spelled word.

Example: (A) everybody (B) every body ______a______

1. (A) alot (B) a lot ______________

2. (A) convenience (B) convenence (C) convienence ______________

3. (A) sanitory (B) sanitary (C) santory ______________

4. (A) jewelry (B) jewlery (C) julery ______________

5. (A) recipient (B) recipent (C) reciepent ______________

6. (A) intermission (B) intramission (C) intermisson ______________

7. (A) evacate (B) evocuate (C) evacuate ____________________

8. (A) pedestrain (B) pedestrian (C) predestrian ____________________

9. (A) idenify (B) identify (C) idintify ____________________

10. (A) intrested (B) innerested (C) interested ____________________

11. (A) perscription (B) prescription (C) prescreption ____________________

12. (A) protray (B) pertray (C) portray ____________________

13. (A) hospital (B) hosiptal (C) hospitle ____________________

14. (A) pertain (B) pertian (C) pretain ____________________

15. (A) repetation (B) repetition (C) repetetion ____________________

16. (A) Febuary (B) February (C) Februay ____________________

17. (A) substitute (B) substitue (C) subsitute ____________________

18. (A) usualy (B) usually (C) usally ____________________

19. (A) offical (B) officail (C) official ____________________

CHAPTER TWENTY-ONE

Using the Right Word

21a
Use the words you mean to use.

21-1 Using the correct word

Directions: Referring to a dictionary when necessary, decide whether any word is used incorrectly in the following sentences. Circle an incorrect word, and write a correct substitute for it in the blank to the right.

Example: In 1953 he had a (fatal) accident that almost cost him his leg. *serious*

1. Ramon had the ideal of giving Juanita a surprise party for her birthday. ______
2. The language of this poem is accepting to all. ______
3. He was shaking from the frightened experience he had just had. ______
4. In Shakespeare's play, Othello portrays a man driven by uncontrolled jealousy. ______
5. My friend Sharon always possesses a sympathetic ear. ______

6. There are many different species of plants that require certain needs. ____________________

7. The change in schedule did not effect me at all. ____________________

8. The boys all love to swim doing the summer. ____________________

9. Put your clothes away neatly in the chester drawers in your room. ____________________

10. Wreckless drivers are a menace to others as well as to themselves. ____________________

11. He kept trying to do the job all by himself irregardless of how many times we offered to help. ____________________

12. The time it took him to get ready was so elongated, we were ready to go without him. ____________________

13. Are you inferring that I'm not qualified for this job? ____________________

14. For best results make sure the line is sufficiently taunt before tying it. ____________________

15. The neighbors have the most humongous dog I've ever seen. ____________________

21b
Use clear or specific words.

21-2 Using specific details

Directions: Rewrite the following sentences so that the meaning is specific and clear rather than general and vague. Try to avoid slang and informal language in your changes. You may need to rewrite all or just part of the sentence.

Example: Because Jerry was carrying so much, he couldn't open the door. Because Jerry was carrying three textbooks, his notebooks, an umbrella, and the garbage can, he couldn't open the garage door.

1. The dog tied to the tree belongs to the main who lives in the house on the corner.

2. Jill is a nice person with a wonderful personality.

3. The room had several plants in various places to add to the atmosphere.

4. There were three colorful pillows on the couch next to the chair by the window.

5. After he ate, Randy left the table a real mess.

6. She looked great in her new outfit.

7. Don's face has features that all go together well. ______

______

8. Cheryl came back from the mall with many things she had bought. ______

______

______

9. The flowers on the table go well with the colors in the room. ______

______

______

10. Jody's dresser top was cluttered with junk. ______

______

11. Marilyn and Henry returned from their exotic vacation to find a pile of mail overflowing the kitchen table. ______

______

______

12. That store sells a lot of nice gift items. ______

______

21c
Use appropriate words.

21-3 Using appropriate words

Directions: In the following sentences underline any slang, regional expressions, informal words, jargon, or clichés. Then substitute more formal standard English for the underlined words. If the sentence has no inappropriate words, write *C* in the blank to the right.

Example: Marvin was so ~~ticked off~~ he slammed the door. angry

1. The guys were rapping about sports and girls and such. ____________

2. She was a real cool chick who could make you sit up and take notice. ____________

3. He was a prince among men, sure to bend over backwards to help a friend in need and, last but not least, one who believed in putting his best foot forward. ____________

4. Marty gets on my nerves because she's all the time trying to rule the roost and acting like the queen bee. ____________

5. Estelle told Wade to cool it and stop making a mountain out of a molehill. ____________

6. Why don't ya'll stop beating around the bush and tell me what you're driving at so I can be tuned in. ____________

7. Mother was really put out when she saw that Tim's room looked like a cyclone had hit it; it was a real pig sty and she was madder than a wet hen. ____________

8. I might could give you a ride if you stay in Chesapeake or Portsmouth, but if your house is in Norfolk, I no can do. ____________

9. Even though I thought he was a swell guy, she gave him the cold shoulder and told him to get lost. ____________

10. You'd better get your act together and turn over a new leaf if you want some foxy lady to notice you. ____________

11. I was shocked out of my mind when you told me they were

engaged; it hit me like a bolt out of the blue, and I'm green with envy since she's pretty as a picture while he's ugly as the day is long. ______

12. He feels like a real jerk since he made such a lousy impression on Linda; she won't give him the time of day. ______

13. Fred worked steadily with great concentration for three hours so that he could finish his homework before his favorite shows came on. ______

14. I wanted to get their input on the problem, but they wouldn't give me any feedback. ______

15. The boss told us the bottom line is we need to increase productivity or some of us may be terminated. ______

21d
Learn how to use these problem words.

21-4 Using a *and* an *correctly*

Directions: In each sentence put *a* or *an* in the blank.

Example: I waited over __an__ hour for you.

1. This is ______ island greatly feared by sailors.

2. Sally is really ______ friendly person.

3. Sam is a person with ______ honest nature.

4. The musicians had guitars, drums, and ______ organ.

5. His goal was to get ______ university degree.

6. I believe that ______________ athlete should be in the best of health, physically and mentally.

7. Meeting you is really ______________ honor to me.

21-5 Using to, too, *and* two *correctly*

Directions: In each sentence fill in the blank with *to, too,* or *two.*

Example: My friend doesn't like to work too long.

1. Do not have the mixture ______________ loose or ______________ stiff.

2. The ______________ boys wanted ______________ come swimming ______________.

3. Try not ______________ follow ______________ closely behind another car.

4. You can't digest your food if you eat ______________ fast.

5. I was ______________ tired ______________ go shopping with the ______________ young children along.

21-6 Using their, there, *and* they're *correctly*

Directions: In each sentence insert *their, there,* or *they're.*

Example: Put your dirty laundry over there.

1. ______________ pride is holding them back.

2. In the room ______________ appears to be adequate light.

3. It is hard to believe that anyone really ever lived ______________.

4. My friends were supposed to be ______________ by six, but I'm afraid that ______________ already late.

5. ______________ going by ______________ house on the way ______________.

21-7 *Using other problem words correctly*

Directions: In each sentence cross out the incorrect word or words in parentheses. Then write the correct word in the blank to the right.

Example: My father is an important man (in, ~~into~~) my life. *in*

1. When this law is put into (affect, effect), the prisoners will be able to decide their own method of punishment. ____________
2. A chill comes over my (hole, whole, hold) body whenever I think of the old Dracula legend. ____________
3. Aside from my mother and sister, no one else comes (in, into) my bedroom. ____________
4. I have a friend (who's, whose) name is Jane. ____________
5. He is the same person (who, which) won the race last year. ____________
6. Travel has changed (alot, a lot) in the last twenty years. ____________
7. When you are on a trip, try not to (lose, loose) time by stopping too frequently. ____________
8. When I walk (in, into) the classroom, I see maps all over the walls. ____________
9. About fifteen minutes later the ambulance arived (to, at) my house. ____________
10. Something which you do (every day, everyday) becomes ____________ an (every day, everyday) event. ____________
11. I was not (all together, altogether) sure we'd followed the ____________ directions correctly until I saw the others (all together, ____________ altogether) at the park.

12. In the (passed, past) I (passed, past) other cars at more than seventy miles per hour, but my (passed, past) driving habits have changed.

13. I have (past, passed) that careless stage in life, and my friends are glad that behavior is now a thing of the (past, passed).

14. There are (less, fewer) people unemployed in this town today than there were fifty years ago.

15. I measured both the children, (then, than) was surprised to find that the younger child was taller (then, than) the other.

16. By the time we were (already, all ready), the bus had (already, all ready) left.

17. (Maybe, May be) we should believe her; she (maybe, may be) telling the truth.

18. We were (all so, also) hungry that we could hardly wait for the others, and when they arrived, they (all so, also) were eager to have the picnic lunch.

19. What is your (idea, ideal) of the (idea, ideal) qualities of a husband or wife?

20. I don't (mine, mind, mined) if (your, you're) not listening to me because you have something serious on your (mine, mind, mined).

21. Sew on that (lose, loose) button, or you will (lose, loose) it, and once it is (loss, lost), it will be hard to replace. ________________ ________________ ________________

22. He resolved to (try to, try and) do better (during, doing) the next quarter of school. ________________ ________________

23. I don't (ever, every) remember his saying he would be there (ever, every) time you needed him ________________ ________________

CHAPTER TWENTY-TWO

Too Few Words

22-1 *Including all the necessary words in a sentence*

Directions: Insert a caret (∧) to show where a word or a group of words should appear in each sentence. Then write the word or words to be inserted in the blank to the right.

Example: When ∧ cake is done, remove ∧ from ∧ oven and cool ∧ on ∧ rack. the, it, the, it, the

1. I am giving you my phone number in case you would like me to come in for interview. ______
2. While walking in the woods, the man disturbed by several gunshots in succession. ______
3. I would always finish my work first, then go to do what teacher requested. ______ ______
4. There were three men were hunting there. ______
5. I have had some experience working in office. ______
6. Mama makes her face up soon as she gets out of bed. ______
7. She told me wait until I was old enough. ______

8. In order to get driver's license, you only need a learner's permit and the final driving test. ______________

9. For some babies, being washed is an experience they rather not go through. ______________

10. My friend asked me to go over her house to see her new car. ______________

11. After you have waxed your floor, let dry for several minutes. ______________

12. My living room is located in front part of my house. ______________

13. If a person bought a used car today, it would cost more money than five years ago. ______________

14. The main reason I enjoyed the basketball game so much because my team won by two points. ______________

15. I am going to tell you how strip and wax your floor. ______________

22-2 Editing for left-out words and expressions

Directions: Edit the following paragraph, inserting any words that the student left out.

A flashlight is handiest electronic invention ever produced. It is also not as complicated. It requires a minimum three parts. The three parts very simple ones: a light bulb that gives off the light, a battery that gives current and voltage to light the bulb, and a switch stops the current flow from the battery to the light bulb. Other items that can improve the flashlight are aluminum foil around light bulb to reflect and direct the light and a colored lens used make signals.

CHAPTER TWENTY-THREE

Too Many Words

23a, b

Do not use the same word too often in a single sentence or short paragraph. Do not use a synonym unless it serves a definite purpose.

23-1 Eliminating unnecessary words

Directions: Cross out any words that repeat something already said in the sentence.

Example: I was running late, and ~~plus~~ I was trying to get my sister ready.

1. Men in our society of today should not be drafted.
2. The pair of twins each wanted the red dress instead of the blue one.
3. In my opinion I think capital punishment will show the public what punishment to expect if serious crimes are committed.
4. Make sure your notes are written down clearly so that you can refer back to them when it's time to review for an exam.
5. The mad, insane people of the world need pity, not condemnation.
6. Jerry was late leaving, so he therefore decided to get gas on the way home instead of before school.

7. I could be learning a trade and plus making easy money.

8. Once the material is cut, you cannot replace it back.

9. First I always assemble the necessary utensils needed.

10. During Easter we usually have the whole family over for dinner on that holiday.

11. Cherie is 5'2" tall in height and weighs about one hundred pounds.

12. Preheat the oven to the proper temperature needed for the cake.

13. Because Joe did not hear what Mrs. Simpson said to do when she first explained, he asked her to repeat the directions again.

14. Leroy had the erroneous misconception that the consensus of opinion of the campers was that we should return back home a day earlier than that which was originally planned.

15. My baby German shepherd puppy ate up all his food and drank down all his water and was still hungry for more food to eat.

16. John and my brother, they like movies in which you can't tell the ending of the story in advance before the movie is over.

17. Separate your eggs apart, then mix together the prepared ingredients, and the end result after baking is a delicious cake.

18. The reason Louise changed her schedule was because she wanted to take the new chorus class in singing.

19. Although I look equally as good in the color green as in blue, my most favorite color is still blue.

20. Personally, in my opinion I believe that by 8 P.M. in the evening, the unintentional

mistakes and inadvertent oversights which almost ruined the new invention will be corrected.

21. In the month of June in the year 1980, the sum total of my high-school graduating class met for a few brief moments in order to prepare for the important and significant events of the coming days.

22. The honest truth is that it is a true fact that each and every one of the ads offering free gifts was deceptive and deceitful.

23-2 Eliminating repetition

Directions: Cross out any words that repeat information already given in the sentence, and substitute for them words that give new information.

Example: If the plants are not watered or ~~are neglected~~, they may wither and die. given enough sun

1. During the church service the preacher preaches to the people the main reason for Easter. __________

2. He is always buying me small, little gifts which have so much meaning. __________

3. Cut off the excess material that you don't need. __________

4. I like my job because I enjoy being around people, and I enjoy typing and taking shorthand. __________

5. I believe the correlation of ideas and thoughts should be used to solve that problem. __________

6. Her ink pen ran out of ink in the middle of the exam. __________

7. Tom and Marilyn enjoy sharing many experiences together owing to the fact that they have similar interests. ______________

23c
Train yourself to say things plainly.

23-3 Stating things plainly

Directions: Rewrite the following sentences in your own words, stating the ideas as plainly as possible.

Example: The theme of the poem seems to be centered around the concept that a fear of insecurity prevails in everyone's mind. *The theme of the poem is that everyone has a fear of insecurity.*

1. Applying the information gathered by psychologists and based on opinions and assertions of my own, I would like to relate my views on the subject of human behavior.

____

____

2. I would like to apply for a job in the field of answering telephones. ______________

____

3. She was considering the question as to whether she should take psychology or sociology. ______________

____

4. The end result of the new program could be crucial to the field of education in our

society today when we are surrounded on all sides by demands for advanced training and knowledge. ______________________________

____

____

5. In this paper I will try to compare high school and college to show that I think they are very different in terms of courses offered, student attitudes, and rules concerning dress. ______________________________

____

____

6. After much advance planning and through joint cooperation, the scientists reached a mutual agreement in order to prepare the very unique new innovation. ____________

____

____

7. We must arrive at a decision at the earliest possible time inasmuch as at the present time we need in the neighborhood of ten additional workers in order for us to complete the job satisfactorily. ______________________________

____

____

8. In view of the fact that we are in a position to offer you another alternative, we hope you will give consideration to the materials sent to you under separate cover until such time as you are able to reach a decision. ______________________________

____

____

____

9. In complying with your request, I am enclosing a check in the amount of $34.97.

10. The biography of his life shows that after a slow initial start, he was able to continue on progressing forward and ascending upward in political leadership positions until he was able to defeat the present incumbent and again restore to the country the same identical prosperity it had enjoyed before.

CHAPTER TWENTY-FOUR
Improving Sentences

24a
Vary the length of your sentences. Avoid a series of short, choppy sentences

24-1 Combining sentences to avoid choppiness

Directions: Vary the length of the following sentences by combining or changing them.

Example: One Tuesday afternoon my son and I went shopping. The first store we went to was Wellman's. We left Wellman's. Then we went to Kirby's. I bought Greg some shoes in Kirby's. Then we looked at bicycles in Ward's. The next thing we did was eat dinner in a cafeteria. Greg and I went to a movie after dinner.

One Tuesday afternoon my son Greg and I went shopping. First we went to Wellman's. Leaving Wellman's, we went to Kirby's where I bought Greg shoes. Then we went to Ward's to look at bicycles. Finally Greg and I had dinner in a cafeteria, and later we went to a movie.

My son is nine years old. His face is clear. His complexion is soft and smooth. His nose is a little sharp and quite long. His cheeks are rosy. His mouth is very small. His lips look thin. His teeth make his smile look very pleasant. His hair is nice and is always in place. His chin is long for a child his age. No matter how he looks, I love him.

24b
Give your sentences a point. Use coordination and subordination correctly.

24-2 Avoiding strung-together **and** *and* **but** *sentences*

Directions: Rewrite the following sentences, giving each one a definite point and avoiding excessive coordination.

Example: The first step in making a dress is to put up your cutting board and fold your material on the right side and lay the material on the cutting board and pin each piece of the pattern on the material separately. The first step in making a dress is folding your material on the right side, laying it on the cutting board, and pinning each piece of the pattern to the material.

1. I don't really know what I may be doing in the near future, but it will be something that I always wanted to be, and what I have always wanted to be is a nurse.

2. My day begins with the ringing of the alarm at 6 A.M., but I don't react to the clock until it rings a second time, and then I dash to the bathroom, shower and dress, and then I rush to the kitchen and eat my breakfast and rush out the door to the bus stop.

3. My mother is a very kind lady, but she's small in size but large in heart and cares for everyone she knows, and she likes to work, but she's a little too old to apply for a job so she stays at home and works there.

24-3 Using **because** *or* **since** *to join sentences*

Directions: Use the word *because* or *since* to join each of the following pairs of sentences. You may want to change some sentences in order to emphasize certain parts.

Example: My favorite radio station is WOWO. It plays rock 'n' roll songs twenty-four hours a day. Because it plays rock 'n' roll songs twenty-four hours a day, WOWO is my favorite radio station.

1. I work the late-afternoon shift. The TV shows I watch are on the air in the morning and early afternoon. ______________________________

____

____

2. Pickerel are fierce fish. Catching them requires extreme concentration and quick reflexes. ______________________________

____

3. Bream are easily caught from shore. Children like to fish for them. ______________

____

4. Every spring the lakes and ponds are crowded with lines thrown here and there like spider webs across the water. Many people enjoy fishing. ______________

____

____

5. I have a few pigeons, an old cat, and a fuzzy-headed dog. I have only a small part of our animal kingdom. ______________________________

____

____

24-4 Using **when, before, after,** *or* **while** *to join sentences*

Directions: Join each of the following pairs of sentences. Begin each new sentence with *when, before, after,* or *while,* and replace the period between the old sentences with a comma. Change capital letters to small letters as needed.

Example: When I go home at one o'clock in the afternoon, I do my homework.

1. I looked for a job for six months. I finally became discouraged.

2. I visited my old neighborhood a few weeks ago. I felt sad about the way the people had let it become run-down.

3. Joan attended college for two years. Her brother served in the U.S. Army.

4. Sue Anne got to the shopping mall at 2:20 P.M. Her mother met her there, and they went shopping together.

5. Steve fished in the surf. His wife enjoyed sunbathing.

6. Tommy goes to school at eight o'clock in the morning. He usually eats a big breakfast.

7. I moved from my hometown. I was sixteen years old.

8. We finished walking in the park. Greg and I went back to the picnic area.

9. Mother washed the clothes. She had already separated them according to their fabrics.

10. Graduation day finally came. Everything in my life suddenly changed.

24-5 Using **if, unless,** *or* **although** *to join two short sentences*

Directions: Use *if, unless,* or *although* to join each pair of sentences below. Put a comma where the sentences are joined if *although, unless,* or *if* begins the sentence. Change capital letters to small letters as needed.

Example: ^Although Ann and Sylvia are sisters~~.~~ ^, they ~~They~~ are not alike at all.

1. An indecisive foreman cannot guide his employees. He gets help from others.

2. Some people work better under a decisive foreman. They should be assigned to his group.

3. Some foremen ignore the needs of their men. Others try to meet these needs.

4. My wife calls me several times each morning. I can't seem to wake up.

5. Sherman is a self-centered person. He usually respects other people's opinions.

6. A sheet-metal mechanic must have a wide knowledge of the various materials and tools used in his trade. He wants to be successful.

7. I turned down all overtime work this semester. I couldn't complete my class assignments.

8. Foremen generally are hard-working people. Like most people, they have their faults.

9. That book had arrived in time for me to complete reading it. I couldn't have written my paper.

10. Enroll in an approved apprentice program. You should want to get more knowledge of your trade.

24c
When you are describing a person, place, or thing, one well-developed sentence is usually better than two short sentences.

24-6 Using well-developed sentences to describe people or things

Directions: Combine each of the following pairs of sentences. Follow the pattern given in the examples.

Examples: Conservative or traditional people find changing their ideas difficult. These people usually belong to the older generation. Conservative or traditional people, who usually belong to the older generation, find changing their ideas difficult.

One of the most beautiful sights I have seen is in West Virginia. It is Smoke Hole Cavern. One of the most beautiful sights I have seen, Smoke Hole Cavern, is in West Virginia.

1. Lamar has a changeable attitude toward his classwork. He is my nine-year-old son.

2. Visual aids make studying history more interesting. Most teachers use them.

3. Modern dancing is one of the things taught in that gym class. I really enjoy modern dancing.

4. Mr. Lewis is an exceptionally gentle person. He is very tall and strong.

5. Boxing is a controversial sport. It has existed for several thousand years.

6. "Tears, Idle Tears" is a short story by Elizabeth Bowen. It's about a young boy who cries constantly.

7. My oldest child is energetic, handsome, pleasant, and bright. He's a boy of fourteen.

8. *Star Wars* was very successful at the box office. This movie is about life in the distant future. ______________________________

____

____

24d
Make your writing more interesting by varying the beginnings of your sentences.

24-7 Varying the beginnings of sentences

Directions: Improve the following sentences by varying the beginning of many of them. Use such words and phrases as those suggested immediately before each group. Notice phrases like *without a doubt, in recent years, for one thing,* and *for another thing* in the example.

Example: Sailing should be considered for youth-oriented summer recreational activities. Several local communities have started learn-to-sail programs. Summer sailing programs are not expensive in our area. Places to sail are abundant. Sailing allows young people to take on responsibilities which help to build character. It's good for almost everyone. Sailing should be considered for youth-oriented summer activities. In recent years, several communities have started learn-to-sail summer programs. For one thing, summer sailing programs are not expensive in our area. With so much water around us, places to sail are abundant.

For another thing, sailing allows young people to take responsibilities that build character. Without a doubt, it's good for almost everyone.

Use such words or phrases as *at least, however, usually,* and *actually*—or similar words of your own—to improve the beginnings of the following sentences.

1. My mother was never a small woman. She's always been heavy as long as I can remember. That doesn't detract from her attractiveness. She's well-groomed and appropriately dressed. Her personality is so pleasant, that's all you'll remember about her.

____

____

____

____

____

____

Use such words and phrases as *to be sure, also, unexpectedly,* and *usually*—or other words of your own—to improve the beginnings of the following sentences.

2. Sailboat racing is good physical exercise. Leg muscles, stomach muscles, and back muscles get a healthy workout when the wind picks up. The opportunity for swimming is ever present. Someone might fall overboard. Such an experience can be great fun for a teenager.

____

____

____

____

____

____

24-8 Varying your writing by using different kinds of sentences

Directions: List the types of sentences in each of the following paragraphs.

Example: (A) Have you ever noticed a police car parked at the side of the highway monitoring automobiles electronically to determine if they're speeding? (B) The device the police officer uses to detect speeders is known as RADAR. (C) Speeding motorists frequently notice the frightening gesture of the officer. (D) "Pull over!" (E) What else can they do? (F) What a relief to get off with only a warning if it's a first offense! b2

A. question
B. statement
C. statement
D. mild command
E. question
F. surprise

1. (A) The American educational system is built around the assumption that every person should be allowed the opportunity to pursue individual goals. (B) Why is education so important? (C) Surely you're teasing! (D) As you know, today's technically oriented society always employs workers with special skills, like those needed for electronics or drafting. (E) In addition, people seeking answers to questions about their government, about ways of improving their lives, and

A. ____________

B. ____________

C. ____________

D. ____________

E. ____________

about interesting and constructive ways of filling increasing leisure time, find these answers in higher education. (F) Why not benefit from it yourself? F. ____________
(G) Enroll in your local community college today. G. ____________

2. (A) Cigarette smokers all have basically the same habits and the same excuses for not quitting. (B) Generally nervous, these people are always searching in their pockets or purses for a cigarette. (C) How disappointed they are to discover that they've just finished a pack! (D) They must drop everything and run to the store. (E) This is an immediate demand! (F) When reminded of the health hazards of smoking, they shrug their shoulders. (G) Don't they realize the risks they're taking? (H) There's no convincing them!

A. ____________
B. ____________
C. ____________
D. ____________
E. ____________
F. ____________
G. ____________
H. ____________

24-9 Writing your own paragraph using different types of sentences

Directions: Write a paragraph of five or six sentences. Make your writing more interesting by using at least three of the following kinds of sentences: statement, command, question, and surprise.

____

____

____

____

____

____

CHAPTER TWENTY-FIVE

The Paragraph

25a
Before beginning to write your paragraph, pick a topic or think about the topic you have been assigned.

25-1 Picking a topic

Directions: Cross out any topics too broad to be developed completely in a paragraph of five to eight sentences, or about 50–150 words. Write *N* in the blank to the right if a topic is not usable. Write *U* if a topic is usable.

Examples: ~~dogs~~ *N*

my dog Sam's friendly personality *U*

1. cats ______
2. my cat's strange behavior ______
3. sports ______
4. my last year in high school ______
5. the highlight of my last year in high school ______
6. Donna, the waitress, at work ______
7. a description of a person at his or her daily work ______

8. my secret hideaway ____________

9. college life ____________

10. the best day I've had lately ____________

11. the day everything went wrong ____________

12. science-fiction films ____________

13. an experience in which I learned a lesson. ____________

14. how to tune an engine ____________

15. how to brush your teeth properly ____________

25b
You should usually begin your paragraph with a topic sentence.

25-2 Recognizing a good topic sentence

Directions: Cross out any items that are not sufficiently limited and correctly worded topic sentences. Write *N* in the blank to the right if an item is not usable as a topic sentence. Write *U* if an item is usable.

Examples: ~~In this paragraph I will attempt to define anger~~. ____n____

Satisfaction is best defined by illustrations of situations in which it occurs, such as the satisfaction of a student who raising his grade from an *F* to a *C* by spending an hour a week in the writing lab improving his writing skills. ____n____

1. How to change a baby's diaper properly. ____________

2. This paragraph will list five simple steps to follow in changing a baby's diaper. ____________

3. If you organize your materials first and keep a cool head and a steady hand throughout, you can change a baby's diaper successfully. __________

4. The best book I've ever read __________

5. Although there are more reasons for attending a two-year college than I could ever cover adequately in this short paragraph, I will attempt to explain some of mine. __________

6. I will always remember the beauty and loneliness of Cape Hatteras, North Carolina, as they appeared to me one autumn. __________

7. A round of golf can be physically satisfying but morally degrading. __________

8. Some people don't like cats, but I do, and in this short paper I will try to explain some of my reasons for liking cats by giving examples of some fine cats I have known. __________

9. How to wash a car without getting wetter than the car __________

10. It is very difficult to define an emotion like love or hate, but that's just what I'm going to try to do in this paragraph. __________

11. I had three main reasons for deciding to return to college __________

12. If you follow these steps, you can succeed in buying a comfortable, properly fitted pair of shoes. __________

25c
After you have written your topic sentence, decide how you will develop your paragraph.

25-3 Recognizing sentences that do not develop the topic sentence

Directions: Write the numbers of any sentences in the following paragraph that do not develop the topic sentence.

My Favorite Cookware

Topic Sentence: (1) *My favorite cookware is old, dented, and handleless, but I love to cook in it.* (2) While some people prefer shiny new pots and pans, I have reasons for my unusual taste in cookware. (3) My old pots and pans look bad sitting on my stove, but I've cooked many delicious meals in them. (4) My friends all laugh at me because I insist on keeping these old battered pots and pans, but they sometimes ask to borrow one of them to use themselves. (5) I don't always agree with my friends on everything anyway. (6) In spite of the hard and heavy use my cookware has had, it still serves me well. (7) In fact, the dents in my boiler and the handle missing from my skillet are reminders of happy times I've spent in the kitchen cooking holiday dinners and special breakfasts. (8) Anybody can buy new cookware. (9) I imagine I'll still be enjoying my battered cookware many years from now.

____

____

____

____

____

____

____

____

____

25d
Use details and examples that develop your topic sentence.

25-4 Using details to develop a topic sentence

Directions: Choose *one* of the following topic sentences; then list five details that might be used to develop it.

Example: Temperance is a very busy and active little girl.
gets into things
makes messes
climbs on furniture
bangs on pan with spoon
sings to herself

1. My first skiing trip turned out to be a disaster. ______________________
____
____
____
____

2. Daydreaming has always been my favorite vice. ______________________
____
____
____
____

3. My father's face, which is wrinkled and rugged, reflects his personality. ______________________
____
____
____

4. I will never forget the house where I spent many happy childhood years.

5. Bathing a baby properly means more than just getting the baby cleaner than when you started.

6. Careful planning can help you to have a successful vacation.

7. My cat, Buster, has a very unusual personality.

8. Observing my dog's routine habits could almost convince you he can tell time.

9. I have a special place I can go whenever I need to escape the pressures of life and renew myself in tranquility.

10. A person can have many different kinds of friends.

11. There are several reasons I chose to attend this college.

12. Organizing a softball game is more complicated than it seems.

25e, f

After you select a method of developing your paragraph, use transitional words so that the reader moves smoothly from one detail to the next.

25-5 Recognizing words that help the reader move smoothly from sentence to sentence.

Directions: In the following paragraph find all the words that help the reader move smoothly from one detail to another. Write these words in the blanks to the right.

How to Prepare a Breakfast of Cereal and Milk

To prepare a nutritious breakfast of cereal and milk, you need to follow only a few simple directions. First, acquire the necessary ingredients and materials: dry cereal of your choice, milk, sugar, fruit, a cereal bowl, and a soup spoon. Second, pour the cereal into the bowl until the bowl is half full. Next, cut up the fruit and arrange it on top of the cereal; then, sprinkle sugar over the fruit, if desired. Once you have layered the cereal and fruit in the bowl, you are ready for the milk. Now, pour enough milk into the bowl to just barely cover the cereal and fruit. At last, your breakfast is ready; pick up your spoon and dig in!

____

____

____

____

____

____

____

____

____

____

____

25g

Make the last sentence complete your paragraph.

25-6 Complete the paragraph

Directions: Read the following paragraph and underline the topic sentence. Then write your own conclusion to complete the paragraph.

How to Put a T-Shirt on a Baby

To put a T-shirt on a baby, be careful to follow some simple steps. First, make sure that the T-shirt is the right size and that it is clean. Then, put one of your hands in a comfortable position on the baby's back, with one thumb under its arm, and raise the baby to a sitting position. Now pick up the T-shirt and put the bottom part of it over the baby's head. Then, continuing to support its back with one hand, use the other hand to pull its arms through the armholes of the shirt. Finally, pull the shirt down and straighten it, still supporting the baby's back.

CHAPTER TWENTY-SIX

The Full-Length Paper

26a
Choose a usable topic.

26-1 Choosing a topic that is sufficiently limited

Directions: Write *U* for usable next to any topic that could be developed in about 300 words during a fifty- to sixty-minute class period. Write *N* if the topic would *not* be usable.

Examples: A lesson I would teach a child ___u___

How to raise a child ___n___

1. How to do the backstroke ______
2. A comparison of education 100 years ago and education today ______
3. Why I consider a certain person a good friend ______
4. The importance of sports in American life ______
5. What I got out of high school ______
6. A comparison of three aspects of elementary school 100 years ago and today ______
7. My life story ______

8. A day I learned something important ____________

9. Three main types of student study methods ____________

10. Breeds of dogs ____________

11. How to overhaul your car's engine ____________

12. How to scuba dive ____________

13. How to change the oil in your car ____________

14. How to pitch a fastball ____________

15. A comparison between Russia and the United States ____________

16. A comparison between renting and buying a home ____________

17. Why world peace is difficult to achieve ____________

18. Why people should not litter ____________

19. Why a student should see a counselor before planning a schedule ____________

20. A review (summary and appraisal) of the classic novel *War and Peace* ____________

21. The character of Mama in *A Raisin in the Sun* ____________

22. A description of the school cafeteria at noon on a weekday ____________

26b
Brainstorm, construct a working outline, and write a good thesis statement for a simple paper.

26-2 Branstorming to arrive at a working outline

Directions: Limit one of the following topics to a subject you could develop in about 300 words. Then, writing for ten minutes without stopping, make a list of all the ideas you can think of on that subject. Cross out any ideas that are not related to your subject, and construct a rough or working outline for your paper.

1. my family

2. cars

3. skating

4. women

5. electricity

26-3 Choosing a thesis statement to suit your purpose

Directions: Each of the thesis statements below could be used in a class paper. Decide whether each would be best for a

des	description
def	definition
comp	comparison/contrast
dir	paper giving directions (process paper)
p.e.	personal experience

Show your choice by writing the appropriate abbreviation in the blank to the right.

Example: My father's face is smooth and gentle. des

1. My mother's face reflects the years of care she has given. ______

2. When I first saw John's den, I thought it was the most unusual room I had ever seen. ______

3. One day I found that my father really understood me. ______

4. Changing a tire is not difficult if you have the necessary equipment, energy, and patience. ______

5. Ice-skating and roller-skating have similar features, but they differ in several important ways. ______

6. Until my first skating trip, I always thought I was a natural athlete. ______

7. The life of a woman one hundred years ago was quite different from that of a woman today. ____________

8. A year ago I had an experience that taught me how to accept responsibility. ____________

9. Good sportsmanship can have many different meanings. ____________

10. Several steps are necessary if you want to write a successful paper for your English composition class: Brainstorm your topic, write the thesis statement, complete the outline, and write and edit your work. ____________

26-4 Using a working outline to guide your paragraphs

Directions: The well-organized paper below appears without paragraphs. Following it is a blank outline for this paper. Read the paper carefully and decide what the thesis statement is and what the topic sentences for each of the paragraphs are. Then write each of these sentences in the appropriate place on the outline. Finally copy the paper, putting it in paragraphs according to the outline.

Caring for Houseplants

Many people today want their homes to be tastefully decorated in natural things. Adding houseplants to homes is a natural and easy way to decorate. Really, nothing can be more natural than nature itself in the form of a houseplant. If plants are properly taken care of, they will help cleanse the air in the house, as well as help to beautify. Taking care of houseplants is much like taking care of children; they all need a lot of attention. An easy way to tend houseplants is to make sure that they have proper food and the right amount of water, adequate light, fresh soil, and clean leaves. You must be sure that the plants are properly fed and watered. Sometimes you may have the notion that water is all a plant needs to survive. However, in most cases this is not true. Like human beings, houseplants need vitamins and minerals, as well as water, in order to grow strong and be healthy. Vitamins for houseplants can be found either in tablets especially made for them or in good plant food. To be sure that your plants are getting the right amount of nourishment, read and follow the feeding and watering directions on the leaflet that usually comes with the plant food. Better still, you can get a book from your library which explains how to feed and water the plants the right way. Proper amounts of food and water add life and luster to the plants, although other things are needed as well. After being sure that you know how and when to supply food and water to the plants, you must be sure that they are getting the proper light. Of course, the best form of light comes from the sun, but there are other forms of light that can do the job almost as well. You might consider getting a grow light or some other commerical product which has been especially made for this purpose. Putting plants in windows that have exactly the right amount of light for them is also important. For example, remember that a cactus can take more light (and much less water) than a Swedish ivy. If the ivy gets too much light, its leaves burn and the plant eventually dies. Probably this is true because of the original environment of these plants. Besides proper food, the right amount of water, and adequate light, another important factor to be considered in growing houseplants is good soil. You cannot allow the soil to become sour, dry, hard, or lifeless. If the soil loses most of its richness, its natural color, and its minerals, the plant should be put into a pot of fresh soil. You can use the same pot if you want to, but be sure to wash it carefully before putting in the new soil. You might want to put the plant into the next larger pot so that its roots can expand and support much healthier and larger foliage. Providing proper food and enough water, having adequate light, and keeping the soil fresh are probably the most important parts of having healthy plants, but keeping the leaves clean and shiny is also necessary. You can do this by brushing off their leaves with a damp piece of soft cloth. Use lukewarm water so that the leaves do not get a shock. Commercial products are also available for cleaning the leaves, but water usually does just as well. However, if you do use a commercial product, be sure to follow the directions carefully. Keeping the leaves clean helps the plant to absorb carbon dioxide more easily. In addition, this helps the plant's natural beauty to shine through. If you follow these directions, you should be able to have lovely houseplants. However, perhaps the most important thing to remember is to treat your plants like children. Plants and children need food, water, light, cleanliness, and attention. If you give them all these things, plants will add to the loveliness and naturalness of your house.

Caring for Houseplants

Thesis statement: ______________________________

____

____

____

I. ______________________________

____

II. ____

____

III. ____

____

IV. ____

____

26c
Practice making a formal outline for a longer paper.

26-5 Completing an outline

Directions: Read the paper that follows this partial outline. Then complete the outline by supplying the needed topics.

Transportation

Thesis statement: Transportation is possible by air, land, or water.

Introduction: ____

____

I. Air transportation

A. ______________________________

B. ______________________________

C. ______________________________

II. Ground transportation

A. Automobile

B. ______________________________

C. Train

D. ______________________________________

E. ______________________________________

F. ______________________________________

III. Water transportation

A. ______________________________________

B. Boat

C. ______________________________________

Conclusion: These methods of transportation are essential to today's world.

Transportation

Transportation provides the means for people to move from one place to another using vehicles designed for air, ground, or water. The use of these vehicles has provided men with the ability to see more of the world in which they live, enjoy a standard of living never dreamed possible before, and, finally, to move outside their own environment into the atmosphere and beyond. The transportation needed for all this is divided into three groups: air, ground, and water.

Air transportation is accomplished through the use of vehicles designed to travel through the atmosphere. This transportation is available through three different methods: fixed-wing aircraft, helicopters, and lighter-than-air vehicles. Fixed-wing aircraft includes those crafts aerodynamically designed with two or more rigid wings that provide lift and stability when ground speed is increased. Helicopters include only those vehicles with rotating blades above the aircraft which are used to provide lift and mobility. The lighter-than-air vehicles include blimps and balloons that use either hot air or gas to provide lift and either small motors or wind to provide direction.

Ground transportation is provided by six different methods: automobile, bus, train, streetcar, motorcycle, and bicycle. Automobiles include personal and commercial vehicles, which carry a relatively small number of people but provide greater freedom for the individual. Buses provide transportation for people to and from cities and suburbs, as well as within areas of a city. In addition, people and small cargo can be carried on buses fairly great distances on land within continents. Trains may be used for people and cargo on short or long hauls. Commuter trains, for example, transport hundreds of people daily. Transcontinental trains carry cargo relatively cheaply. The streetcar is similar to the bus, but this mode of transportation is not especially popular anymore, except as a tourist attraction. Motorcycles provide transportation for a limited number of people, too, especially in the United States. However, they are also used by many people in other countries.

Water transportation is provided by three methods: ship, boat, and hovercraft. Ships are large, floating, citylike structures that can carry hundreds of people over long distances. Boats, on the other hand, are usually somewhat smaller floating craft that transport people and cargo on rivers or other inland waters. The hovercraft, a somewhat new concept of travel, uses helicopter, aircraft, and ship design techniques to provide a stable, high-speed water transportation mode for small groups of people.

These various methods of transportation are essential today. The ability of people to travel and send cargo throughout the world gives them a sense of freedom, allows them to enjoy other cultures, and normally provides their economy with large numbers of jobs. However, the largest single advantage of efficient transportation methods is a better standard of living for most people. Can you imagine a world without vehicular transportation?

CHAPTER TWENTY-SEVEN

The Library Paper

27-1 Using the card catalog and preparing bibliography cards

Directions: Use the library catalog to locate any three of the subjects given below. For each subject, select two books and prepare bibliography cards for them.

Code names
Emergency medical services
American ballads
Barter
Television and the family

27-2 Using indexes to magazines and preparing bibliography cards

Directions: Locate any three of the following subjects in *Reader's Guide to Periodical Literature.* Choose two articles for each subject selected and prepare bibliography cards for them.

Dog training
Mortgages
Plant propagation
Hairdressing
Levi Strauss
Dandelions
Professional baseball
Noise pollution

27-3 Preparing note cards

Directions: Using the paragraph below as your source, complete separate note cards for each exercise that follows: (Use the publishing information from this workbook for your bibliography card.)

Air transportation is accomplished through the use of vehicles designed to travel through the atmosphere. This transportation is available through three different methods: fixed-wing aircraft, helicopters, and lighter-than-air vehicles. Fixed-wing aircraft includes those crafts aerodynamically designed with two or more rigid wings that provide lift and stability when ground speed is increased. Helicopters include only those vehicles that have rotating blades above the aircraft which are used to provide lift and mobility. The lighter-than-air vehicles include blimps and balloons that use either hot air or gas to provide lift and either small motors or wind to provide direction.

Thomas C. Cooper

1. Use three words in the first sentence in a direct quotation as part of another sentence.

2. Summarize the third sentence.

3. Using appropriate lead-in phrases or clauses, directly quote the second sentence.

4. Again using appropriate phrases or clauses to introduce them, use six or seven words from the last sentence.

5. Summarize the entire paragraph.

6. Complete the bibliography card.

27-4 Preparing note cards and making an outline

Directions: Locate a short article on a subject of your choice. Prepare two or three note cards for the article. After completing the cards, make an outline that includes the central idea, main headings, and subheadings.

CHAPTER TWENTY-EIGHT

Putting the Paper in Final Form

28-1 Proofreading and correcting

Directions: Proofread the following paragraphs. Mark and correct any mistakes.

Example: The first week in july was so cold that my vacataion was ruin. When I went too the beach. I had to wear a coat all of the time.

(1) My First Day in College

Last monday was late registration day for College. I came up school early because I thought that registration would only take a few minutes, and I could go right to my classes. I work on my schedule without knowing that some of the class were closed, and then I had to start all over again. There were too difference offices to go through after the forms were completed. And both of them had long lines. Late registration is, a problem; next time I am going to register Early.

(2) "Should Teachers Curve Grades?"

Many student is relieve when a teacher curve the grades on a test, maybe they didn't study, or they couldn't rember enough to receive a passing grade. A grade which has been curve can help these student, but for most persons it do more harm then good, the curving of a grade can have a damage affect on a students furture progress.

First of all, when a teacher announce that the grades will be base on a curve. The student know that he don't have to study as hard. If everyone else study as much as he do. If a student study very hard and get a high grade. It will mean the other students will get lower grades and he will be dislike by those students.

Also, a student might fail to learn some important information. In a two-year course. A student be expect to know everything in the first year before they continue to the second. If the teacher curve grades. Perhaps that student will not learn every thing, and he may find hisself loss in the second year.

Teachers should not cruve grades there may be a good reason to curve them at the time, but in the long run, it will harmed the student.

CHAPTER TWENTY-NINE

Writing Business Letters

29-1 Learning to write a business letter

Directions: Using the block or the modified block style, write a letter of complaint in response to the following problem.

You and your family were recent guests at the Beachview Hotel at Lookout Beach, California 96728. Several unpleasant things happened during your four-day stay. To begin with, the hotel had no record of your arrival date, despite the fact that you had confirmed reservations. As a result, you had to wait four hours for two adjoining rooms. In addition, you had asked for rooms overlooking the ocean. These rooms were unavailable until the third day of your stay.

After you returned home, you received a final bill. On that bill you noticed charges for goods and services you had not received: $28.32 for room service and $2.25 for delivery of the daily paper.

Address your letter of complaint to Mr. Thomas Snow, the hotel's manager.

29-2 Learning to write a letter of application

Directions: Using the block form or the modified block form, write a letter of application in response to one of the advertisements below.

> PHOTO LAB TECHNICIAN MANAGER For new business opening in area mall. Experience in color photo finishing. Exciting opportunity to work with processors such as Nuritzu, Copal, Oriental, etc. Write to P.O. Box 4135 care of *The Morning Advocate*, Bristol, Virginia 29885.

REFRIGERATOR MECHANIC Full & part time. Top pay, all benefits. Send letter of application and resumé to Howard Lewis Refrigeration Services, 832 N. Smithfield St., Bristol, Virginia 29855.

SECRETARY-RECEPTIONIST For solo medical practice. Send letter of application and resumé to P.O. Box 8242, Mountaintop, Virginia 29745.

SOCIAL WORKER Permanent part-time position in long-term geriatric setting. Degree & experience preferred. Send personal data sheet and application to P.O. Box 4832, *The Morning Advocate*, Bristol, Virginia 29855.

SECRETARY For construction estimator. Must be experienced. Write to P.O. Box 1319 care of *The Morning Advocate*, Bristol, Virginia 29855.

The application letter on the following page was written in response to the advertisement below. Use it as a model.

MANAGEMENT ANALYST Applicant must have experience improving managerial effectiveness. Minimum requirement: associate degree. Send personal data sheet and application to Mrs. Jean Walton, Personnel Director, Management Consultants, Inc., Vienna, Tennessee 32609.

2555 Town Point Road
Suffolk, Virginia 23435
January 6, 1984

Mrs. Jean Walton
Personnel Director
Management Consultants, Inc.
Vienna, Tennessee 32609

Dear Mrs. Walton:

I recently read your advertisement in *The Daily Call* for a management analyst. I am seeking just such a position, and I believe that my qualifications fit the requirements of your advertised position.

On June 10, 1983, I shall graduate from Tidewater Community College with an Associate degree in Management. I have supplemented my education with other training courses which I have listed in the enclosed data sheet. In addition, I feel that the awards I have received indicate my ability to perform duties over and above that which is normally expected.

I have four years of supervisory experience and have managed an office independently for four years. During the past year I have worked as a management analyst for Doctors' Hospital in Portsmouth, Virginia. In this position I provide advice and service to managers in planning work methods and procedures with the objective of improving managerial effectiveness. I conduct interviews, collect factual information, and prepare management studies on my own.

The enclosed personal data sheet provides more detailed information concerning my background and qualifications. I am available for an interview at your convenience. I may be reached at the above address or by telephone at (804) 738-2147 after 5:00 PM.

Sincerely yours,

Darlene P. Jones

Darlene P. Jones

Enc.: Personal data sheet

29-3 Learning to write a personal data sheet

Directions: Using the headings below as guides, complete a personal data sheet which you can include with your letter of application in Exercise 29-2. (The data sheet that follows has been completed to comply with the letter of application for the management-analyst position.)

Name

Address (street, city, state, ZIP code)

Telephone (area code) (complete number)

Position Sought

EDUCATION

College, Date of graduation or of pending graduation

Degree

Honors or special activities

High School and Date of graduation

EMPLOYMENT EXPERIENCE

Date of your employment with the most recent first | Job title and responsibilities

REFERENCES

Darlene P. Jones
2555 Town Point Road
Suffolk, Virginia 23435
Telephone (804) 738-2147

Position Sought: Management Analyst

EDUCATION

Tidewater Community College, Portsmouth, Virginia. Associate degree in Management expected in June 1983.

Academic Honors:
- Member of Phi Theta Kappa Honor Society
- 3.65 grade point average in Management courses (on a 4.0 scale)

June 1974, graduated from Central High School, Portsmouth, Virginia.

Academic Honors:
- Graduated in top third of class
- Received Outstanding Service Award

Extracurricular Activities:
- Member of Yearbook Committee
- Member of Homecoming Committee
- President, Theta Sorority

EMPLOYMENT EXPERIENCE

January 4, 1983 to present	Management Analyst, Doctors' Hospital, Portsmouth, Virginia Supervisor: Mr. E. James Provide advice and service to managers in planning, organizational structures, work methods and procedures with the objective of improving managerial effectiveness. Prepare reports of findings, analyses, and evaluations of accumulated facts and suggest internal changes in work methods to increase efficiency. Conduct interviews to collect factual information. Apply basic management and analysis knowledge in performing work assignments. Prepare management studies with minimal supervision.

January 8, 1979 through January 4, 1983	Administrative Assistant, Doctors' Hospital, Portsmouth, Virginia Supervisor: Dr. M. Smithson Served as Administrative Assistant to the Chief of the Obstetrics and Gynecology Department. Provided direct supervision and other managerial responsibilities for four civilian employees. Coordinated statistical data collection and reported information as required. Served as central contact point for interpretation of hospital and departmental guidelines and instructions for both staff and patients. Coordinated and reviewed all incoming and outgoing correspondence, records, and reports for the department.

ADDITIONAL TRAINING

May 5-6, 1982	16 hours	Word Processing – Training on the Lanier LTE-4 Norfolk, Virginia
May 20, 1982	4 hours	Prevention and Detection of Fraud Waste, and Abuse, State Hospital, Portsmouth, Virginia
June 6-11, 1982	40 hours	Work Simplification and Methods Improvements (creative problem solving and simplifying work procedures), Norfolk, Virginia

SPECIALIZED EXPERIENCE

Employed as a real-estate agent on a part-time basis (25 hours per week) for four years. Gained additional knowledge in communicating with others. Gained experience in financing practices, realty practice, laws, contractual documents, and maintaining my own income statements and balance sheets.

AWARDS

July 23, 1983 Superior Performance Award Doctors' Hospital
September 22, 1982 Outstanding Performance Evaluation Doctors' Hospital
June 5, 1981 Appreciation Award, Syntex Labs., Inc. U.S. Navy

OUTSIDE INTERESTS

Member of the Beta Sigma Phi International Women's Sorority from 1976 to present. Served as Secretary and Treasurer of the Beta Xi Chapter.

REFERENCES

Furnished on request